Praise for Messages from the Spirit Realm

"This beautifully written book offers an interesting view on life and death. Reflecting on my own experience when my son died in a tragic accident, it made me think about how I handled my grief (not very well). It is a very thought provoking and at times confronting piece of literature. "

Sonia Michaelson, Australia

"In my reading of June's book, *Messages From The Spirit Realm*, it certainly gave me a deeper understanding of life on Earth. While we might question those who ask for a horrific death, maybe in a former life they were the perpetrators and needed to come back to move on? If we could all be in this realm, kind, loving, understanding and giving, maybe we could create "Heaven on Earth?" It's a book you can't put down. "

Audrey Long, Australia

"I found this book to be very informative and it gave me a wonderful perspective of the different Spirit Realms. It has made me look at passing over in a very different light.

I now understand that no matter what happens in the future, everything is predetermined before we arrive and to make the best of the journey I am on.

I would recommend this book to anyone who wishes to understand more fully about grief and passing over. "

June Mitchell, Australia

"This book is a wonderful resource for anyone who is seeking additional information, or a different perspective, on some of life's challenging situations.

Whether you are already in alignment with this particular way of thinking or not, please take the time to read and absorb the information. It may just resonate with you in a way you never thought possible, as we never know when a window of information and understanding will open within us.

This book may just be the catalyst to assist you on the journey. Enjoy.

Lorraine Mill, Australia

"As a reader you don't have to believe in the Spirit World to enjoy June Redfearnes' books. Everybody can relate to the topics the Spirits have chosen to talk about through Junes' hand. The style is light and the explanations easy to understand. This gives the reader an understanding of crises that occur through this journey of human life, and can help to overcome grief and tragedy.

These messages are quite philosophical and of interest to everyone who wants to make the most of life on Earth."

Elisabeth Enz, France

Messages From The Spirit Realm

THE COMPLETE SERIES OF 5 CHANNELLED BOOKS

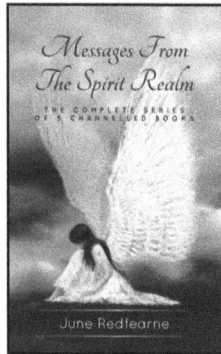

June Redfearne

Artwork: Laila Savolainen

Spirit of the Boabs

National Library of Australia Cataloguing-in-Publication entry

Author:	Redfearne, June, author.
Creator:	Redfearne, June, author.
Title:	Messages from the spirit realm : the complete series of five channelled books / June Redfearne ; Laila Savolainen, illustrator.
ISBN:	9780995395220 (hardback) 9780995395244 (paperback) 9780995395237 (ebook)
Subjects:	Channeling (Spiritualism). Guides (Spiritualism). Spiritualism. Angels. Heaven.
Other Creators/ Contributors:	Savolainen, Laila Kristina, 1967- illustrator.

Publishers Details

Spirit of the Boabs (ABN 89378673394)

Contact Details: info@spiritoftheboabs.com

Kununurra, Australia

Contact: Sarah Brett

Interior and Cover Layout

Pickawoowoo Publishing Group

Printed & Channel Distribution

Lightning Source | Ingram (USA/UK/AUS)

~

The author can be contacted through the publisher:
info@spiritoftheboabs.com
www.spiritoftheboabs.com

From Spirit
With Love

Foreword

I feel deeply honoured to have been involved in the production of this series of books, Messages from the Spirit Realm, which have been channelled by my beautiful friend June Redfearne. June has been a friend for nearly twenty years and it was not until she sent me her first manuscript for assessment that the Universe directed me into publishing.

It has been a long and winding road that has led us to create this collection of 5 books and I would like to thank June for her great patience and perseverance along the way. It has been a steep learning curve for both of us, but we have trusted that Spirit would guide us along the correct path, as they have done.

I know that the time is right for this information to be shared with humanity, so that those with uncertainties about the presence of Spirit in their lives may have their fears dissolved. May these *Messages* encourage you to live your life as I have for many years now, knowing that Spirit are always there to help and support us at all times......all you have to do is ask.

With love

Sarah Brett

Spirit of the Boabs

Author

I am the 'Writer' of these books, not the 'Author.' All I know of the Authors is that they are beautiful Spirit Beings; that I know some of their names and that I have their blessings and their love. I feel honoured they have chosen me to write this information to help my fellow Man.

I became a Spiritual Healer many years ago and was first introduced to automatic writing in 2006 by a dear friend of mine Audrey Long. I was told shortly afterwards that I would write a number of books. I had to wait until the Spirit Beings advised me that I was ready before I could begin channelling this series.

I have been through many hardships in my life, but was told that I needed to go through these so as to be experienced enough to write this information. My message is: "No matter how old you are, don't give up the dream of one day doing your part for the good of your fellow Man and know we are all Children of the Universe and very much loved."

I would like to sincerely thank the Pickawoowoo Publishing Group ladies for all their help, patience and sage advice during the creation of this series, and Laila Savolainen for her beautiful artwork for our covers.

June Redfearne

Contents

Messages From The Spirit Realm

A CHANNELLED BOOK

June Redfearne

Messages
from the
Spirit Realm

Rellman, Yellmean, Jeanette, Jeremy and other Spirit Beings will relay information through June.

Please believe this information.

Please glean this information.

Please allow this information to be of great help.

Spirit Beings have emphasised some words and not others. It has been channelled, recorded and presented to you as it is here with approval from Spirit.

Understanding the Process

———————— ❧❧ ————————

Spirit Realm is another name for a place where people go when they pass over from the Earth Plane. Spirit Realm is a place of great beauty and peace where people go when they leave the Earth Plane either after being very sick, or from old age, or accidental death of some kind. Very sick people and those who have committed suicide go to a place we will describe as a mezzanine heaven, where they will heal before going on to the higher Spirit Realm.

Messages from the Spirit Realm (This is the title of the books they have given me) is a series of books channelled through June so that they can be published in order to help people understand what happens when people pass over from the Earth Plane to the Spirit Realm, where family and friends meet after passing over. Many people do not understand about the Spirit Realm, so they have no peace after the death of a loved one.

The connection between the Spirit Realm and the Earth Realm is energy. The process after someone leaves the Earth Plane is as follows: only the body is placed in the Earth, but the person's energy still lives on around the people they love. The energy stays with their loved ones and their Soul carries on to the Spirit Realm. Many people still feel the energy of their loved ones long after they have passed.

The Spirit and the Soul are two different entities. The Spirit is what carries us to the Spirit Realm and the Soul is what inhabits the Spirit Realm thereafter.

When people pass over to the Spirit Realm they are at first unaware that they have shifted from the Earth Plane to the Spirit Realm. It takes some reassurance from their loved ones, who have passed earlier, to make them realise they have passed from Earth Plane to Spirit Realm.

Newly passed over people can take some adjusting to their new surroundings – allow them some time before their Earth family and friends try to make contact, because until the recently passed over Spirit has adjusted, no communication can get through.

Once the adjustment has been made, gallant efforts will be made by the newly passed

Spirit Being to try to make contact with Earth family and friends. Many Mediums can also make contact between the Earth Plane and the Spirit Realm

Earth people need to understand that their loved ones are not lost to them. There is a thin veil between the two Realms that can be crossed when the time is right.

This information is being written in an uncomplicated way, in order to help people understand this process. Complicated descriptions and explanations can be very confusing when trying to come to terms with the loss of a loved one and unnecessary pain and grief can result from the thought that loved ones are gone forever.

If only people could understand how very close our loved ones still are, then a lot of disillusionment would be taken out of their lives. There would be a lot less pain and anguish and their grieving process could be a lot shorter.

A person who keeps grieving does not allow their loved one to move on. Once they are able to move on, and the quicker they are allowed to move on, the quicker contact can be made with the loved one.

Holding on to grief for a long time causes the passed over loved one the need to be closer to the griever, so they are therefore unable to go to the higher Spirit Realm, where they can heal and be at peace.

❦

Losing Children

People who lose children are more likely to grieve for longer and these forlorn people tend to be unable to feel anything other than the pain of losing their child. Their pain will also be of greater depth, as parents are of the understanding that they are not meant to lose their children before the parent leaves the Earth Plane.

In the greater picture, everybody chooses when they leave the Earth Plane and this is decided before they come to Earth.

Parents feel in a very precarious situation and can feel guilty about losing a child and wonder if they were to blame in some way. This adds to the burden of their grief and therefore it takes longer to come to terms with their child's death.

So close is the bond between mother and child, not just physically, but spiritually and energy wise, that it is very difficult to break that bond, even when death occurs. This is when parents could accept the death sooner, if they realised that their child is not lost to them.

The parents are the carriage to bring the child into the world and that child is meant to be here for a specific purpose, which is usually unknown to those who love them, therefore it seems a huge sacrifice to have the child taken.

Another Myth

Another myth to dispel is that the people who pass over are unhappy. It is the people who are left behind who feel the pain. People who pass over feel like they have arrived back home and they feel very blessed that they have come home. It is a myth that we pass over and are unhappy, in-fact they are feeling very happy about it.

People who keep grieving are spending much precious energy on their pain, so if they can accept that their loved one is very happy, they may feel some relief and be somewhat happy for their loved one.

This is not to take away the reality of their loved one's death, because what we feel is a natural human emotion. People who understand the happiness of their loved one coming home can hopefully shorten their grief and begin to rejoice in the happiness and peace of their loved one.

People are always going to remember and love the person who has gone home. It is our reality to be able to see and touch and talk to other people and, when we are not able to do this, we feel that we have lost our loved ones for good.

A way to believe our loved ones are not lost to us is to talk to them anytime we feel the need to have contact. Please realise passed over people can hear us and will try to respond.

Denial

─────────── ✤ ───────────

People who are personally connected to the passed over being are more likely to be in denial about what has happened to their loved one. These people do not always believe their fellow beings that the passing was ordained long before the passed over being came to the Earth Plane.

There are many different ways people will handle the passing of someone close. Denial puts them in a place where they don't have to cope with the passing. This places a great burden on the loved one left behind to cope with the passing of their relative or friend, which places a great strain on their lives.

Please remember to not take the burden on your shoulders, as this was the choice of the passed over being, who is now very happy and at peace.

Getting Past Grief

— ❧❧ —

If people cannot get past their grief, they permanently keep their loved ones tied to them, so that loved one cannot move on to the Spirit Realm. This makes many people unhappy, the passed over loved one and the grievers.

People who grieve for a long time may themselves become ill, as grief can become an affliction in itself. It doesn't do anyone any good if the death of a loved one causes another sort of death and that is the death of the loved one who is left behind. Another sort of death means the sickness of the left behind people. The sickness causes the left behind people to lose their way of life, which is like a death in itself. It is the death of their normal life and can therefore interfere with their home life, family life and work life.

Earth bound people are bound by earthly feelings and it may be difficult for them to realise the beauty of their loved one's going home to the Spirit Realm. No matter how much we want them to understand this, their earthly feelings will stand in the way for however long they feel it necessary.

Imagine how much the loved one who has passed cares for his or her family and friends left behind? So much so that they are continually keeping watch over the Earth people and helping them in any way they can. This is why it would be so much easier for the departed person to make contact if people of the Earth Plane could grieve less and open their hearts to the possibility of a connection between the two Realms.

Many people are coming to grips with the idea of connecting Realms and it is those people who will impart the reality to those who are still in the dark about this connection.

Wouldn't it be wonderful if Earth bound people could open their hearts to what has already been written? The majestic place of love, which is the Spirit Realm, could become much closer.

Murder

⟡

We must touch on the subject of murderers and the murdered. This is a profound experience for both the perpetrator and their victim.

It is extremely hard for Earth people to comprehend that this is a forgone decision before coming to Earth. Like any passing, it is decided long before being born. Please allow some time to comprehend this statement.

It places the perpetrator in a very horrific situation knowing that they have been chosen to take someone else's life. This statement can be very controversial, as Earth bound people are repulsed by the sadistic nature of these killers.

It would be absolutely the hardest thing to accept that your loved one has chosen such a terrible demise, but please try to understand that they have chosen this for themselves. It is a contract between the two parties before leaving the Spirit Realm to come to Earth and it would take their Earth families a very long time to come to grips with the idea that their loved one chose this.

There will be a lot of anger and hate towards the perpetrator by the victim's family and, unless they can come to understand the dynamics of this process, no amount of explaining will make a difference.

This is a subject that may need to be read some time after the action of murder, before the family has any chance of understanding the process. Their departed family member will be watching and waiting. The departed loved one, who has been murdered, keeps reminding their families that it was their choice to pass over by being murdered.

It may take their family a very long time to be able to get this message from their departed loved one, as the families' grief will overshadow any other emotions they may have and will not allow any messages from their loved one to come through for a very long time. This is why it is very important to try to come to terms with the situation as soon as humanly possible, so that the message from the passed over loved one can come through sooner and allow their family to realise their loved one is not lost to them.

It will be almost incomprehensible for some people to even imagine this sort of death was chosen, especially when there is more than one perpetrator. Each of these people means to go through this experience so that they can move on to a Higher Realm. This is not to say that everybody has to go through some sort of horrific experience to be able to go to a Higher Place. It is only those who choose this, so they are able to go to a Higher Place sooner. Some people feel the need to move faster.

Although it is a subconscious thought, the ultimate goal of the human race is to reach the Spirit Realm, their home.

Once the murdered person has reached the Mezzanine Heaven, they will stay there until they have overcome the trauma of being murdered, when they will go on to the Higher Realm.

The perpetrators have sometimes been contracted to murder other people and it is only when their contract is finished will they finish killing. This is also true of paedophiles that harm children. This is also a contractual thing between the two parties before coming to the Earth Plane.

In the eyes of the human race there is no excuse for the actions of these perpetrators. This is why this book must be written to explain why these things happen and hopefully human beings of the good kind can see past these horrific events and realise it is all predestined.

Spirit Beings do not expect Earth bound people to be accepting of this because it goes against all humans believe in, but these books aim to explain how these things come about.

Once the two parties, the perpetrators and their victims, are in the Spirit Realm together, the passed over murdered person or persons will thank the perpetrator for carrying out their wishes while on the Earth Plane. Once again, this is incomprehensible to Earth Plane people and in no way are they expected to be okay with this, but hopefully, they will realise that it is no one's fault that these people were murdered and this understanding may help take away any guilt they carry about not taking enough care of their loved one when on Earth.

Greed

❧

Greed puts people in a place where they are so busy trying to get as much money as possible and not caring how they get it, who they hurt to get it or where they get it from, that they cannot lead a normal life.

People who are greedy and who feel compelled to gather as much money and material things together, exclusive of all other normal activities, find at the end of the day they may become very lonely people. There is no doubt they will have people around them, but quite often it is to participate in the wealth of the greedy person. On a personal level loneliness can set in.

These people are here to learn generosity towards their fellow Man and whilst they insist on gathering material possessions, this lesson will never be learnt.

Greedy people come to the Earth Plane with a feeling of scarcity, which perhaps comes from another field of their existence. This is why they have chosen to come to the Earth Plane to go through this experience of greed and to learn that money and possessions do not necessarily make people happy. People go through many existences, all of which teach us something each time.

Greed is only one such experience and one that must be dealt with before there is any chance of becoming a whole person.

Jealousy

Jealousy can be a very debilitating emotion and can cause a great deal of harm within people's relationships. As mentioned earlier, when people leave the Earth Plane their energy remains around those who love them. People are made up of energy and, when fellow human energies are used by being jealous or hateful, it can interfere with, or destroy, the Soul.

Soul-destroying energies are neither beneficial nor constructive in a person's life. Jealousy
and hate can eat away at a person's personality and character and can retard their journey
to the Spirit Realm. We all come to the Earth
Plane to go on a journey and to learn lessons
to take us to a Higher Place. If we don't seem to
have as much as others it is pointless to be jealous, or hate someone for it, because we have
chosen this path for ourselves to take us on a
particular journey through life.

Some of the hardest paths chosen are the
ones which will take us to a better place sooner,
not meaning that we will die earlier, but when
we do pass over, we may not need to come
back again, or we may need to come back
fewer times.

Hardships are really a blessing and it would
be wonderful if Earth Plane people could open
their hearts to this and know that there will be
greater rewards on Judgement Day: Judgement
Day meaning our arrival in the Spirit Realm.

Trauma

Trauma, along with grief, jealousy and hate, can be very debilitating emotions. Trauma keeps people from being happy and content. Trauma is sometimes an unavoidable situation and can be caused by many different events.

The most common trauma is trauma of the heart, which can be the most crippling of all traumas. Bodily trauma may take time to heal, but trauma of the heart is the hardest to come to terms with. Trauma of the heart places a human being in a very precarious situation because trauma changes the way people think and feel. When people suffer trauma they are not in any position to make rational or wise decisions and a lot of their decisions will be made out of pain and anger. People may place themselves in a place of confinement, so that their lives are interrupted from functioning normally and therefore their Soul does not function properly. The human being's spirit is broken. Allow time for the Spirit and the Soul to heal.

Please know that the pain will pass and that the Soul and Spirit will keep functioning as intended when the trauma has passed. Trauma of the heart is mainly caused by losing someone by death, separation, by feeling we have done wrong by someone, or when we feel we could have done something more in some way.

Trauma is very much like grief and can significantly interfere in our lives. People who have trauma of the heart can sometimes take as long to heal as someone who is deeply grieving. Trauma is like grief and, as explained earlier in the book, by understanding the dynamics of the Spirit Realm, grief can be shortened.

Trauma of the heart can place us in a situation where we can learn a very valuable lesson. It is not to say that we are being punished by having trauma of the heart imposed upon us, but learning how to cope with it teaches us a very important lesson that we have come to the Earth Plane to learn.

Trauma is only one way we can learn valuable lessons.

Fear of Death

Fear of death keeps people's minds on dying, rather than living. They can sometimes be afraid to live properly for fear they may cause their premature death.

We want to take away the fear of death and try to educate people that death can be a wonderful experience, even for those who have a traumatic death. At the moment of death, however we die, comes the most wonderful and beautiful experience. The humans' Angels and loved ones come for them and don't allow them to suffer any more than tolerable, especially when a person has a traumatic death.

The person who is passing over is wrapped in a blanket of love and peace and is taken to wherever they need to go, either to the Mezzanine Heaven to heal, or to the Higher Plane. As explained before, the passed over being can sometimes take a while to realise they have passed over, but at no time do they feel that they are alone. They will be taken great care of until they feel at peace with their passing.

The only difference with our relationship with the passed over person, is that we cannot see and feel them physically. We can still communicate with them as we normally would when they are well enough to be contacted.

What a wonderful gift to the passed over loved one to be out of pain and to feel the best they have ever felt. How could we take that away from them, especially when they have suffered greatly on Earth, or have had a traumatic death?

It is a human emotion to feel great loss, but our passed over loved ones help us in any way they can to get us through this time. We are human and we go through human emotions, that is partly what being human is about and part of our journey on Earth. Hopefully, this passage will take away some of the pain and allow us to be happy for our departed loved ones.

Suicide

─────────── ৵৵ ───────────

People who commit suicide readily leave the Earth Plane for the Spirit Realm.

People who commit suicide are placed in a situation of great distress, which becomes so unbearable that they cannot cope with human existence any longer. Suicide recalls a lesson the human comes to the Earth Plane to learn. It is not to say what that lesson is, because it is only known to the suicidal person. They know what they came to learn, (subconsciously) and as soon as that is fulfilled they feel it is no longer necessary for them to be on the Earth Plane. They don't recall what the lesson is from the Spirit Realm, but subconsciously they feel it is time to go.

This way of leaving the Earth Plane is chosen by the person before leaving the Spirit Realm. They put themselves in a situation on the Earth Plane where problems and way of life causes untold stress, which leads them to commit suicide. Allow suicide victims time to heal in the Mezzanine Heaven before trying to make contact. Usually, the passed over person will endeavour to make some sort of sign or contact to let their loved ones know that they have healed and are ready to be contacted.

The suicide victim has chosen their parents and their way of life, which eventually leads them to suicide. This once again removes any guilt from their family or friends that perhaps they could have done more to prevent this occurring.

By saying the suicide victim chose his or her parents, and way of life, which would eventually lead to their demise, does not mean the parents, or how they lived, had any bearing on why the loved one committed suicide. It simply means that it was a situation that they chose to be in, because events in and around that situation would cause their demise so they could fulfil their wish to suicide and pass over that way. It was simply their way of going home sooner.

If a person has ordained their suicide, then very little can be done to prevent it.

People who attempt suicide and survive have asked for intervention from the Spirit Realm and therefore survive the attempt. This means they have learnt a valuable lesson, even if it is unknown to them by human standards, but choose to stay longer on the Earth Plane. Those who achieve their suicide mission are ready to go home earlier.

❦

Old Age

⚜

This chapter is about the people who are not meant to go to the Spirit Realm until old age. People who grow to old age are here to teach others the value of life and to impart their well-earned wisdom on to those who need some guidance.

A lot of people don't always heed the advice of an older person because they think the older person does not know what they are talking about. However, somewhere from their rich tapestry of wisdom, gleaned through life experiences, comes a trickle of wisdom that may somehow get through.

There are people we call Earth Angels whose specific role on Earth is to guide and comfort others in need of help. Earth people don't always recognise the Earth Angels because they look and act like everyone else. The reason for that is so that they can function on the Earth Plane while they carry out their work. A lot of people who have experienced hardships throughout their lives can also become Earth Angels. Allow these people to be of great help to you.

Earth Angels often turn up when help is needed and it can sometimes seem like a small miracle; please know these people have been chosen to carry out this sort of role.

If only Earth Plane people could realise that all they need to do is ask for help and it will come in some form, even though it may not be how it is expected. Sometimes it can be a very small miracle and hardly noticeable and, if our problems seem insurmountable, we may not notice it at all. Other times it will come in a much bigger way and that may be the only time we realise we have been given a miracle.

This passage has been written in the hope that whoever reads this will open their hearts and minds and realise help is available.

As written in earlier paragraphs, people who are murdered, commit suicide, or who die from some other cause before what Earth People call 'their time', will go to the Spirit Realm as planned when their ordained time comes. No matter what earthly help they ask for, their Spirit Realm wish will be granted. However, before their chosen time to go to the Spirit Realm comes, they can also receive help for other things, if only they ask.

(Message to June)
Rellman wants June to keep faith in what is channelled for these books. People will be receptive to this information because it is needed for people to understand and to cope with some situations.

Abortion

❧⬥❧

Abortion plays a big part in some people's lives, whether it be a direct connection, or by association. Please understand abortion plays a big part in the scheme of things.

The guilt and trauma that can go along with abortion can be catastrophic for some people and it may remain something to feel guilty about for the rest of their lives. Nothing happens on Earth without there being some other plan, something in the larger scheme of things.

There can be fear of persecution for aborting a foetus and some people worry that it may be a crime against nature or God. People, who keep feeling guilty about aborting a foetus, need to know there is nothing to feel guilty about. Just know that an aborted foetus' Soul goes back to the Spirit Realm, just as any other Soul would who has actually lived on the Earth Plane for however long it might be.

The Soul of the foetus has hardly had time to forget anything it knows from the Spirit Realm, therefore it is quite happy to be going back so soon. The Soul of the foetus only needs that short time in the womb of a human to know what it is meant to learn. It is only when a baby is born that it forgets everything about the Spirit Realm. While it is still in the womb, knowledge of the Spirit Realm is still fresh in its mind.

When people abort, they feel they have made the decision themselves or someone associated with them has made it for them. Know it is a decision made deep within their mind, because subconsciously they know it is time for the foetus to go back to the Spirit Realm. If someone else has made the decision for the pregnant person, then that someone else has been put in the pregnant person's life to make the decision for her deep from within their mind. The aborted foetus can at some time re-enter the Earth Plane, as there can be another lesson to be learnt.

Everything that happens on Earth is part of the big scheme of things and it is all ordained.

We all have very deep knowledge within us from Spirit Realm and it is from this deep knowledge that we make decisions. Some people make decisions that they themselves do not understand, but know it is what is meant to be. The decisions of everyday living are usually made from the Human mind, but the decisions made that affect somebody's life are ordained before leaving the Spirit Realm.

Potential

This passage lets people know about their potential on Earth. Everybody has very deep knowledge within them brought from the Spirit Realm.

Each person has the potential to do great things on Earth. The only thing stopping Earth people reaching their highest potential is the way they choose to live their lives and the way they think. None of this will ultimately change the way we have chosen to leave the Earth Plane, but while we are here, people could achieve great things.

Many people feel the need to know more, and although they are not sure what they are searching for, this will often lead them on a find and discovery search. It is these people who will ultimately be of great assistance here on the Earth Plane. Many people succumb to the temptation of Earth living, such as too much drink and too much of the Earth vices, so that they are unable to reach their full potential while on the Earth Plane. However, some of these people, who have gone down the path of vice, have, after seeing the light at the end of the day, become of great assistance on the Earth Plane. This also relates to people who choose great hardships for themselves (as explained earlier in the book) so they can learn very important lessons and put them to great use.

If only Earth bound people could see how much deep knowledge they have within them, then they could become so much happier on Earth. This would allow them not to worry so much about hardships, as they would know the great rewards that would come with it.

Please do not continue to incur further hardships and sickness so that we glean sympathy from other people, this will never allow us to move on. As mentioned earlier, we can ask for help in our daily lives and we will receive it in some form or other if we keep an open mind. This also goes for people who constantly want to be sick or in hardships so as to receive sympathy or help from their fellow man. The wish for wanting to be sick or go through hardships will also be granted.

People who come to Earth with an affliction from the Spirit Realm have chosen to do this before coming to Earth and therefore may live the rest of their lives this way. These are not the people who want to gain sympathy from others, but it is those people who are sick and who could heal more quickly but are not inclined to want to because of the attention they receive.

How wonderful it would be if we could tap into this deep knowledge we all have within us. This can be achieved by keeping an open mind, being kind and thoughtful toward our fellow man and by stilling our minds long enough so as to reach deep within to be able to find the deep oasis of knowledge we have there.

Rewards

What a wonderful thing it is to realise that we can all reap rewards for things we have done on Earth and for the way we choose to live on Earth.

Rewards are not only for people who lead blameless lives, but they are also for people who have been through many hardships. The rewards are of the heart, which means people can feel so good about themselves that they are much happier and therefore have a better life. People who feel happy that they have done some good have an open mind and that is when their rewards come to them.

People who have many hardships are able to understand others who are also going through hardships and their empathy for others can also gain them rewards. People who are happy attract so much more into their lives. Their minds are full of happiness and love and that can only bring more of the same.

This is not to say we can feel good all the time. Humans have to live an Earthly life and with that comes hurdles we all need to cross, but if people can keep a positive mindset, then life could be so much better. Hardships and hurdles are instances where people can ask for Spiritual help and by doing this the burden can be eased. The more our burdens are eased, the happier we become, therefore people are well on their way to leading a rewarding life.

Many people will still go through hardships that can almost be unbearable, but remember, help is available and every little bit of help we receive can ease the burden.

People have a choice of how they think about their situation. On the one hand they can see it as a horrible affliction and never be happy, or they can see the good and positive in certain situations and therefore are much more content with their lives.

Humans come to Earth to learn lessons and if enduring hardships is part of it, then so be it, but please remember we are never forsaken and help is always available if only we care to ask.

Releasing

Releasing means letting go of any guilt or responsibility that people may have over the demise of someone close to them. People can carry guilt for the rest of their lives if they are not relieved of this burden.

Their whole life is concentrated on what they could, or should have, done and no matter how bad they feel, they need to know that no matter what they did, it would not have changed the outcome.

Everybody leaves the Earth Plane when and how they choose and that is why it is imperative for people to unburden themselves of any guilt about the part they played in the lives of the departed. It cannot be stressed enough that people play a big part in their own problems. It is their internal thoughts that can keep them trapped in an unhappy life.

Releasing means letting go of any guilt or negative thoughts. Give any burdens one may carry over to the Divine and be free to live a peaceful and fulfilling life. It is alright not to be laden with guilt. People cannot carry out their role on the Earth Plane if they are trapped in guilt and worry. Remember our loved ones are happy, at peace and how they wish to be.

Any loved ones who have gone on the wrong path (as humans may put it) have chosen this way of life before coming to the Earth Plane so as to learn important lessons. Some may take a whole lifetime to learn, while others learn very quickly and are able to go on and help their fellow Man.

Please free oneself of the responsibility and know all will be well in the big scheme of things.

Pleasing Other People

So much of our time and energy can be spent trying to please other people. Some people spend a lifetime putting their own needs aside to please someone else. This is a human failing and one which happens so often in life. Please understand other people's needs and wants are no more important than your own.

Some of us are made to feel inferior by people around us and therefore we feel we need to accommodate their needs before our own. This comes from a feeling of inadequacy on our part. Unfortunately, by doing this, our time on Earth does not accomplish anything for ourselves.

The only way it will work, is if we finally discover the futility of being there for others all the time and not doing for ourselves. This in itself can be a very worthwhile lesson. If only we could understand this sooner and realise when Earth people feel worthwhile, then that is when so much more good can be done for others.

A person who is feeling inadequate, who is doing for others, never really achieves anything. A person who feels very worthwhile can achieve so much good for others, because it is coming from a place of wisdom, rather than a place of inadequacy.

A person receiving help from an inadequate feeling person never really learns anything either. Rather than doing for themselves and learning from the experience, they allow someone else to do it for them, therefore nothing is learnt.

The Taker, and the inadequate feeling Giver, get caught up in this situation and neither gets to learn valuable lessons, which can take them to a Higher Place.

All our circumstances are different and, although sometimes our actions do not show it, we are all equal in the eyes of the Universe.

Our Souls are pure, if only our human hearts could learn to be the same.

Balance of Life

Balance of life means people need to try to balance their lives out so as not to have more stress in their lives than happiness and peace.

Right back to the beginning of life there has been stress and in small doses it can be very beneficial. Stress can create adrenalin and adrenalin is what keeps us going in times of need. When life began on Earth, adrenalin is what kept people safe in dangerous situations and it is still so in this time of life.

Stress can also be caused by people worrying about things that may not have even happened yet, but which they anticipate could happen. These are times when, if only people could still their minds, they could ask for Spiritual intervention and guidance. By doing this they can bring some calm back into their lives and therefore they can find some peace. There is a time for stress and adrenalin and there is time for peace and happiness. Even people who have constant hardships could have some peace, if only they could allow themselves time to be calm and ask for Spiritual intervention.

Life on Earth was never meant to be easy, otherwise we would never learn anything. There must be a balance, so that people can have some calm time and this is when a person's thoughts are clear and are able to make rational decisions for the benefit of themselves and those around them. It cannot be stressed enough that a calm and peaceful mind is imperative for our existence. A mind which is in turmoil all the time functions from an internal source and nothing is seen beyond that.

To smell a flower or to hold a loved one's hand are only two very small deeds we can do to bring some peace of mind. There are so many small deeds we can do to help with the process to bring calm. What a magnificent thought that such a small thing can bring so much joy and harmony to a person's life and in return so much rationale for us to be able to function properly.

So please be stressed if necessary, but make it a short-lived process and then turn to the inner place of beauty and peace. Open your hearts and accept the Divine help that is there for the asking.

Random Acts of Kindness

All through the many lifetimes there have been people who have done Random Acts of Kindness. A Random Act of Kindness is something a person does on the spur of the moment. Other acts of kindness can be something that has had a lot of thought put behind it. Whichever way it is, both are equally blessed by the Universe.

An act of kindness or thoughtfulness can have a huge impact on levels of energy that circulate on the Earth Plane. Often a small act of kindness can have a domino effect and one act of kindness can lead to many others. An act of kindness can mean the healing of someone's heart and can restore faith in human nature. Sometimes it is more profound than an act of generosity, because an act of kindness comes from the generosity of the heart.

How simple would it be if Earth Plane people could comprehend that there is Spiritual help and guidance for the asking and love and understanding towards their fellow Man can help heal the troubled Soul? There would still be many lessons to be learnt, but how much easier would life be and how much more able a person would be to cope with the hurdles of life, if their fellow Man showed some kindness and understanding?

This will not change the deeds some people are put on Earth to perform and, although it is incomprehensible to Earth Plane people that they can perform these acts against their fellow Man, wouldn't it be wonderful if

Earth Plane people could show them even a small amount of kindness and understanding? Many people would prefer to hate these perpetrators, but that turns within and can create bitterness and unhappiness, so it is within our power to forgive.

Even though it would be very hard to understand why this happened and even harder to forget, what a wonderful gift it would be to ourselves and our loved ones to show forgiveness.

The Magnificence of the Afterlife

It is beyond the comprehension of Earth Plane people to know the magnificence of the Afterlife. It is especially designed this way, otherwise Earth Plane people would want to get back there as soon as possible and would not spend enough time on Earth to learn anything. The magnificence of the Afterlife is a heart soaring and profound experience that would be impossible to describe in all its glory.

It could only be explained in a simple way to Earth People and it can be experienced in a simple way by opening our hearts and letting in the love and beauty of life and, in return, giving out as much love and beauty as we feel. This is only a tiny example of how it is in the Afterlife.

It is so magnificent, that it is the hardest decision for a Soul to make to come back to the Earth Plane for another lifetime lesson. This may help to explain why a foetus, which is aborted, is very happy to go back.

A lifetime could be a few short weeks in the womb, or several decades of life on Earth. Both are a lifetime for the Soul. A lifetime does not necessarily mean a full lifetime in human terms, but any time with life is considered a lifetime, be it short or long. This is why, as explained before, it is every human's subconscious goal to go back home to the magnificence of the Afterlife.

People Who Relate to the Spirit Realm

———— ❧ ————

Blessed are the people who relate to the Spirit Realm. These are the people who connect the rest of Earth Plane people to the wonders of the Spirit Realm. These people are teachers and healers and servants of the Universe. They teach people to reach out to the wonders of Life and the Universe in all its glory. Their hearts are open and their minds are clear and they are here to help the many, many more people who are willing to learn and carry on the wonderful work of the Earth Angels.

The more people learn and love and open their hearts, the sooner they and others around them can heal. Their journey to the Afterlife, their home, the Spirit Realm, will be complete.

So, from tiny foetuses in the womb, to old age, there is a huge range of living and learning and loving and doing, and sometimes the journey can be long and tiring and arduous. Just know from the information gleaned in these writings, that the burdens of life can be lightened by asking for help, by showing love and kindness towards their fellow man, and by being willing to accept Divine love into their lives for now and always.

Please allow yourself time to process,

absorb and accept this information.

Please know this information is true and correct.

Let these *Messages* be consolidated

within yourself before you move on

to the next book.

Messages From The Spirit Realm

THE NATURE CHILD

June Redfearne

Messages
from the
Spirit Realm

Rellman Yellmean, Jeanette and Jeremy and
other Spirit Beings will relay information
through June for the book "The Nature Child".
The Spirit Being Yellow Feathers from the
Crow Tribe has also come through
with some information.

Please believe this information.

Please glean this information.

**Please allow this information to be
of great help.**

The Nature Child

The Nature Child is a very special little being, who is sent to Earth to teach people the value of love and peace between Man. The Nature Child is recognisable by their angelic look and peaceful nature. They have come from the Realm with a definite mission. The role of these children is to make all people look at life through their eyes. Some have special gifts and others have a rapport with animals and nature. Whichever way it is, they have a deep knowing that most of the human population does not understand. They have a deep insight into life and some adults may quote as saying: "old heads on young shoulders".

The Nature Child personally relates to animals and insects; they relate to the world of Nature. They are happiest when they are with animals and nature and they have an affinity that most people don't understand. This is not to say many people do not have a love for nature and animals, but the Child of Nature's depth is much more profound.

A Child of Nature is pleased to be able to bridge the gap between people of the normal thinking and the profound depth of knowledge of the Nature Child.

The Nature Child feels different from other children; they also look different from other children. The nuance of difference in their looks is subtle and may not be noticeable to the mainstream population. Their hearts are pure; they are happy and funny and loving and lovable. These children cannot understand how Man can be unkind to each other and to the nature that they love so much. Some of these children are born as Down's syndrome children and sometimes can be the most loving.

Whenever people are near the Nature Child, their energies change and they become calmer. They can almost feel the love coming from the child, which in turn makes them feel better.

These children are our hope for the future. They will grow into adults who will love and respect the Earth and her nature. Their intention will be to save the Planet rather than destroy it. There is no malice, jealousy or greed in these children, therefore their purpose will be pure.

There has been so much destruction on Earth through Mans' greed and want of power that

Nature has been torn apart in the process. Man has forgotten the importance of Nature, which is imperative for our survival.

Man has destroyed so much of the Earth that it will take a long time to repair some of the damage. Unfortunately, it will be a mammoth task to get some of them to see what needs to be done. This can only be done with love and understanding and this is where the Nature Children come in. It will be a task beyond com-prehension initially, but as time goes on and more Spirit Children join the Earth Realm, the easier it will become.

The basis of life is Nature, without it the world cannot exist. It is a god-given gift to Man and Man has taken it to destruction. There is only one hope of saving the planet and that is if humans amend their ways and begin to heal the Earth. It will take a flood of Nature Children from the Spirit Realm to start the process. It takes one drop of water to start an ocean and that is how this will work.

This book is written in the hope that each reader can see the value in the healing process and may be able to contribute to its salvation. Save one tree, one plant, one animal and the process begins.

Magnificent the mind, magnificent the Earth.

Plunder the mind, plunder the Earth.

Mother Nature keeps replenishing herself but it can be a merciless job when Man keeps destroying her.

Material objects

We may wonder why half the Earth relies on production. The Earth keeps production of material things to provide man with unnecessary objects that can well be done without. The more material things the more destruction. Greed rules Man so much that he is blinded to the harm that is being done to the Earth Realm.

Man is born an innocent child. Better than anything is the innocent child. The child is born unadorned with no knowledge of greed or want of power. Unfortunately, most grow up to learn the want of material objects. It seems a normal process to them and a rite of passage.

The Nature Child comes to Earth with none of these expectations. Their only desire is to save and love the Earth in all her glory.

The Nature Children choose their parents, who perhaps in some way are pleased to co-operate with the child's beliefs of saving the Earth from destruction and therefore allow the child their uttermost ideas without interference.

God also anticipates Man will destroy his own race if things are allowed to continue the way they are. Man has created many diseases and illnesses with inappropriate food interference. Man has created toxic air that we breathe. Man has destroyed beauty of landscape and waters, all to benefit his own greed and power. Man's only needs are food and shelter and love for one another.

Many challenges would still face Man as he needs to learn many lessons to be able to go on to the Afterlife.

Man in all his misguided wisdom keeps pleasing himself and forgetting there is a Judgement Day. This does not mean Man will go to hell, as there is no hell, only what Man creates. Judgement Day is for Man to know how far or not he has come and how far he needs to go to create his own Heaven.

Man may need to come back many more times until he can stand in the glory of the Universe as a whole and beautiful Soul. How clear it could be if each person opened their mind and looked deep within, there to find their salvation.

How simple life could be. Simple, beautiful and pure.

Fear of Hell

Many go to church and have hell and terror rained down upon them for being sinful according to the law of the land. Humans have, for a very long time, been ruled and bombarded with the fear of Hell.

We would like to take away the fear of Hell, as Hell can only exist in Man's mind and at times Man has made his own Hell on Earth.

Church can, and should be, a place of peace and fulfilment. Please be guided to find a place of Worship that offers the peace and calm Man so desires.

Fear not for Salvation can be yours. Salvation does not mean God will come to Earth to save us. Salvation means Man can save himself.

The Spirit Realm has blessed us with the Nature Children and it is now up to Man to redeem himself and the Earth.

The Existence of Man

The existence of Man can be a very complicated and complex process. No one on Earth would be able to comprehend the journey Man takes unless they themselves remember their time in the Spirit Realm. We can only hope that each person, each time on Earth, can become a better person and embrace the love showered upon them from the Spirit Angels.

Each time on the Earth Plane brings Man closer to his ultimate journey's end, where he can bask in his own salvation. Retribution can play a bit part in Man's journey on Earth. He may feel the need to pay some debt from his last incarnation and he can make this choice before leaving the Spirit Realm. In other words, if Man has performed some awful deed on Earth, such as murder, he can redeem himself in his next life if he so chooses. Even though he was chosen for the role, he feels the need to live a better life next time around and therefore do some good on Earth.

Not too much more can be explained about Man's journey through time, as it can be very intricate and not easily absorbed by modern Man. Just know there is an answer to everything and a reason for everything no matter how complex it may seem. Unfortunately, because of the world the way it is today, Man's purpose has been lost and greed and want of power has crept in.

Guilt can place a Man in a situation where he can perhaps feel the need to provide more material things for his family so as to allow them to be on a level with their counterparts. He can sometimes unwittingly go against his own principles to achieve this goal. Maybe a statement can be made by doing this but if only he realised how futile this can be and know it is taking him further and further from his goal and purpose on Earth.

Suffice to say: whatever Man chooses to do will be far reaching into the future. Should he choose to heal the Earth then Mankind will have a future. Should he choose to continue the way he is then the Nature Children will have a very hard job ahead of them to turn things around.

Time is of the essence and time could be running out for Salvation. The ultimate plan is to have peace on Earth and it is a right of Man to have peace. The only thing getting in the way is Man himself.

Electronics

We must touch on the subject of electronics. Electronics have taken away the ability to communicate with one another, another invention of Man to put him further behind in the quest for ultimate peace. It must be said that some of these devices can be very helpful in the search for healing diseases, however most diseases are created by Man in the first place. Had not this been so these electronic devices would not be necessary and so it becomes a vicious cycle. Man needs peace to function and there is no peace forthcoming in the world of electronics.

Voices from the Spirit Realm cannot be heard when they are blocked out by constant noise; noise and electronics sever the connection between Heaven and Earth and so once again the Nature Children have a monumental job on their hands.

Comprehension of the Nature Child

————— ❦ —————

Can Man ever comprehend the value of these children? Comprehension of the Nature Children will take some time and in turn it may take some time for things to turn around.

Many people are on the path to help save the Planet but these people need the help of the Nature Children who are being sent to Earth for this particular purpose. Amazing things can be achieved with love, patience and respect. Respect for each other and respect for the Earth itself. Man has, in the past, been the cruelest animal on Earth. Animals only fight and kill for survival and supremacy to ensure the continuity of their species. However, Man has been cruel for greed and power.

What a wonderful world it could be if greed, power, cruelty and hate could be taken out of the equation in our lives on Earth. It is so unnecessary for any of these vices to exist. Man could have everything he wants by loving and caring and sharing with his fellow Man.

Please know this is possible in time to come and know it is in the power of the Nature Children to bring this about.

When we leave the Earth Plane we leave behind our energies. What a wonderful gift it would be to our loved ones to feel the energy of the departed as a loving energy and not an energy of self-absorption. Take one minute of every day to give rather than take and the axis begins to shift in favour of a peaceful existence.

If only we knew how much spiritual power existed in each one of us. Man has used his earthly power to control. How much more beneficial it could be if Man used his Spiritual power to love.

We must remember some Souls return to Earth to carry out deeds contracted before leaving the Spirit Realm and these deeds will be carried out regardless of anything else. This does not mean the rest of Mankind needs to carry out deeds of selfishness and cruelty. These are traits learnt while on Earth and are not ordained behaviour.

The Nature Children or Spirit Children, as they

can sometimes be known, have chosen to come to Earth knowing their task is monumental and we must be grateful for that.

❦

The Second Coming

—————————— ❧ ——————————

*T*his passage was very powerful and rather daunting for me to write and I had to take a minute to absorb it. As a matter of fact, I did not really want to write it at all. However, Rellman (my Angel) asked: "Please June write the information as it is being channelled." (Seeing I am only the channel and not the author of these words I have obliged).

The Second Coming is not God or Jesus coming to Earth and healing our existence and us. The Second Coming is Mankind, helped by the Spirit Children in their infancy and adulthood, turning our lives around and recreating the Earth as it is meant to be.

This may go against the beliefs of some religious people, who believe Jesus will resurrect and come back to save us, but know we are watched over by the Divine at all times and if this is Jesus, or God, or the Universal Love, then so be it.

Please know there is no need for any guilt for any deed done on Earth. Just know we need to mend our ways if peace is to reign. What has been done cannot be changed, but what is about to be done can be changed. The Nature Children will help bring that about.

Lost Souls

When peace on Earth can be felt, many departed Souls, who have lost their way, can once again be reunited with their loved ones, who have passed earlier. Lost Souls have been through a dark time on Earth. Allow them some peace. When peace on Earth reigns they know it is time to move on. They will learn their dark place does not really exist and any connection with the Earth Plane will dissolve, because there can be no dark place when there is peace. Also Man will learn there is no dark place when peace reigns.

Souls in dark places mean they have not crossed over completely and are still connected to the Earth Plane, because they are confused as to where they should be. They are lost Souls for the time being and need our help; they need us to let them know it is time to go to the Spirit Realm and it helps if there is peace on Earth.

Anytime we can be calm and at peace it would be a gift to the lost Souls to talk to them and reassure them it is time to go. This can only be done with love. Once again the Nature Children can help bring calm.

This must be a separate reality to ordained deeds and contracts made between Souls before coming to Earth. These can be very dark deeds, but these too can be helped by people forgiving and knowing in time there will be peace.

(At this point I have asked Spirit to explain about Souls in dark places more clearly so that readers can understand.)

What we consider lost Souls are Souls who have not found their way to the Afterlife, as some traumatic event has kept them close to the Earth, so therefore they have not yet found peace. This is what we may consider hell or purgatory and this is where the thought that there is a hell may come from. This is why it is important to have peace on Earth, so as to allow the lost Souls to be able to move on. If there is no trauma on Earth, then there is nothing to keep them here.

As mentioned before, trauma creates a dark place and, if there is no dark place, there is nothing to keep the lost Souls close to Earth. The other thing that may keep them close so they are not able to move on, is their loved ones grieving too long. This creates trauma for the lost Souls and the left behind loved ones.

If people can be at peace with the death of a loved one, after a normal grieving period, then the Soul is free to be at peace. Our departed loved ones will never forsake us, so we have no need to hold them close to the Earth.

Attachments

Attachments can mean when a Soul makes an attachment to a human being because the Soul may feel it is lost. An Attachment can feel like a bad energy and that is because the Attachment is taking away some of the human's energies.

These are some of the entities we referred to earlier in the book as lost Souls. However, it is only occasionally a lost Soul will attach to a human. This is why we can sometimes have an eerie experience, with the feeling that someone is close by and making us feel bad.

Many Souls are lost and don't know where to go, but it is the Attachments that need to be encouraged to move on more so than the lost Souls. They all need to be encouraged to move on, but it is imperative for the Attachments to be removed from human existence as soon as possible.

This can be done with encouragement, love and patience. The Attachments are very scared and need a lot of assistance and reassurance to move on. It helps to be calm and at peace to allow the Attachments to know that there is no need to be afraid and that they need to go on to the Spirit Realm to meet their loved ones, who have passed before, where they can be healed.

Attachments also means the Soul is traumatised and keeps on clinging to the human body. This is why it is important to be always calm and assure them it is time to go and for them to know how happy they will be.

If we feel we have an Attachment it can sometimes be of help to invite a Medium to identify the Soul and help it understand it needs to move on to the Spirit World to allow itself and the human it is attached to, to both be free and happy.

Spirit is waiting for them and ready to embrace them into the Hereafter, to be loved and cared for and to take their fears away.

Relationships

─────────── ❦ ───────────

We may wonder why some people have one relationship or marriage through their life, while others are destined to have many partners, and yet others may not have any at all. It is all a part of the big scheme of things, where each relationship teaches us something new. The ones who stay in one relationship for life and who are happy, have been through many lifetimes and have become Soul Mates. These people don't need to learn anything new about being a partner, but still may need to learn other lessons and need to be with their Soul Mate to do this.

People who stay in lifetime relationships and who are not happy are there to learn the lesson of loving themselves and not always doing for others. We must love ourselves before we can do good on a conscious level for others.

People who have many partners are meant to learn something from each relationship that will take them on a discovery journey of who they are. Some of these separations can be very painful, but even the pain can take us to a new realisation. We are not meant to grieve or be traumatised for too long over a separation. The quicker it can be dealt with, the quicker we can move on. Please know the pain will pass and we can go on to the next phase.

Those who only have short relationships, or those who don't have any, are the Earth Angels who are here for the greater good of Man. By this we mean they are here to do the work of the Universe and perhaps need to find what that work is before they can feel complete. A relationship may then enhance their life.

We are not meant to feel guilty over what we do or have done in our lives; we are meant to learn from it and, if our deeds are painful to others, we may need to learn to change our ways.

Mortality

Mortality can weigh heavily on some people's minds. Some may feel they will pass from the Earth Plane before they have discovered their true purpose, or feel they have not achieved enough. This could mean material things, achievements or discoveries. Know whatever we have become or achieved in our lives before we pass over is what we are meant to achieve. Be it a little, or a lot.

Each lifetime is a learning process and, contrary to some beliefs, we have the chance to come back to the Earth Plane and continue our journey of discovery. We would like this Earth to become a place of peace and tranquillity, so it is a much nicer place to come back to when ready. This is the purpose of the Nature Child.

Many do have a very specific role to play on Earth and sometimes it can take almost a lifetime to discover this. A specific purpose is one of Teacher, Healer or dispenser of Wisdom. The reason it can sometimes take almost a lifetime is that some need to go through many different experiences in life to learn the wisdom, so as to go on to help others. Some of these experiences can be catastrophic at times but it is a well-earned lesson and a great gift to pass on to others.

Many people know early in their lives their purpose on Earth. These people have been here many, many times before and are almost to their journey's end, meaning their journey back to the Spirit Realm. These are often referred to as "Old Souls".

The most profound journey is the journey inwards, deep within the Heart and Soul to the core of our being. From this comes the love and forgiveness every Man needs.

Remember mortality becomes immortality as we as Souls live on in the glory of the Universe.

Manifestation

Manifestation can be done almost anywhere merely by meaningfully creating in our mind what we want from life. The Universal love is there to support us in whatever we may want.

This means if we have lost our way gallant efforts will be made to help us create anything we want, if we can be positive and do it with a loving heart. No good can come from us trying to manifest something that is not for the good of all concerned. We will go against our own judgement if we try to create something that may coerce someone else or go against someone else's wants and wishes.

Life could be so simple in some ways, such as manifestation that can be for the good of us and those around us.

Manifestation does not mean our life's path will be changed, but it can enhance our existence as it is. A small example of this is: we can manifest more peace in our lives but it does not change the course of our lives, it just means it will enhance our lives.

How fortunate we are to have the most powerful essence in Spirit supporting us in what we want.

This does not come without some effort: we cannot just want something and hope it will come about. We must put some effort into creating a positive and beneficial manifestation and it must be for the good of ourselves and all who are connected. Keep an open heart and positive mind for what we want and live as though that change has already come about.

Rewards can be most gratifying when effort and love from the heart has been put into it. It cannot be stressed enough that Spirit is waiting to help whenever we need it, even if this comes in weird and wonderful ways, as Earth Plane people would put it.

The Spirit Children are here to try to change the Earth for the better and we can change ourselves in small ways to help to bring that about.

Doors closing

A door closing can be a hugely painful experience to begin with and it may take some time to come to accept that it has happened, but a door closing on something that we thought we really wanted can sometimes be a huge blessing in our lives. Once again Spirit works in weird and wonderful ways.

The first reason this can be a blessing is that a very big lesson can be learnt from this experience. It is a lesson of learning to cope with pain and disappointment (as it can be with many painful experiences).

The second blessing is that it can be a lesson learnt that can be passed on to someone else and can be beneficial in their lives.

Spirit does not give us anything we cannot cope with, such as pain and trauma and catastrophic experiences. These can be the greatest gifts of wisdom that cannot be gained in any other way.

These words may seem simple and trivial

when we wonder why so many terrible things happen. Happenings, good or bad, are our learning journey and we have chosen this before coming to the Earth Plane.

Spirit cannot prevent these things from happening, but Spirit can be there to lighten the burden of the pain and prevent us from going through too much pain and suffering before our demise, as in the case of a traumatic death. This is why it is said that Spirit will not allow us to go through more than we can bear. Please know that Spirit is with us at all times, so that we can take heart that they will step in when the time comes.

A door closing can feel like a death. It can hurt almost as much as a great pain caused by monumental events. Spirit wants us to know that the death of one thing can mean the rebirth of another. We may at times hold on to the old for too long and miss the door of opportunity on something new.

Magnitude

The magnitude of life can be overwhelming at times and we can become lost in its vastness. We can become confused as to which way we should go. It is these times when we need to quieten our minds and look within. We can afford ourselves a few minutes of inner peace to find the answers to whatever is troubling us.

We brought with us a magnitude of knowledge from the Spirit Realm when we re-entered the Earth Plane and it is from this knowledge we can gain our solutions.

We must try to learn to live in the Here and Now and not become overwhelmed by the magnitude of life. The Here and Now allows us to be present within ourselves and therefore find some peace and solitude.

Blessed is the time when the Nature Child has done her work and blessed we will be when peace reigns on the Earth Plane. The Nature Child brings with her a magnitude of knowledge and from this knowledge can teach us (if we will listen) the love and patience that is needed to bring calm to the Earth Realm

(It is at this time that the Indian Guide named Yellow Feathers from the Crow Tribe decided to come in and have his say.) His message is as follows: "Yellow Feathers wants June to know that there are Indian Nature Children who will help bring calm to the Earth Plane."

Spirit had told me there are Nature Children all over the world, but Yellow Feathers is the only Guide so far who has been able to come through at this time to let us know about the Indian Children (Bless his heart). My thanks to Yellow Feathers.

Justification

Unfortunately, a lot of people, who do not want to learn, are continually justifying their actions. Justification gives them a sense of entitlement to go on living the way they have always done and therefore they feel there is no need to explain themselves.

The Nature Child will have the hardest job with these people, because they feel they have no need to change their ways and, no matter what they are told, they will stick steadfastly to their old habits. We as Spirits work very closely with the Nature Children and hopefully eventually some crack will show in the armour of these steadfastly stubborn people.

Once again, it brings to bear the mammoth job the Nature Children have. We must be so grateful for their existence and their willingness to help bring peace to the Earth Plane.

Maybe these stubborn people will have a very important role to play if they can be shown a better way to treat the Earth Plane. Their stubbornness and determination, which was once used for things other than the good of the Planet, can be a very useful tool for working for the good of the Earth.

Justification has no place in the scheme of things if it is used to benefit those who are determined to keep putting the Planet in jeopardy because they can only see rewards and greed for themselves.

It is in the hands of the Nature Children, with the help of Spirit, to bring things back into balance.

Emotions

Emotions can cancel out any other purpose. People live by their emotions and emotions can, at times, prevent people seeing a clear picture of what is reality.

Having emotions is human. They are what we have when we are happy, sad, grieving, angry and an array of other feelings. We need emotions to be human. We need emotions to love and love is the most important emotion of all.

The Spirit Children will try to teach humans to overcome any negative emotions and concentrate on the emotion of love. We must point out that other feelings are important also, but some would be better controlled, such as anger and hate.

How damaging is anger and hate to a humans' energies? These energies suffer trauma with negative emotions and can create an illness that could otherwise be avoided. It only takes a feeling of hurt or betrayal and it can control our lives for a very long time. It is only a human emotion and we have the power to dismiss it. We have an endless oasis of love deep within and it is there for the asking.

If only we could see that the power of love can overcome almost anything and it is in our power to do so.

Realisation

Some people are already beginning to realise that the balance needs to shift if we are to save the Earth. Unfortunately, there are too few of these people so it is timely that the Nature Children have come into existence. Many people, who have realised the situation, find the task too daunting to even attempt to make some changes.

These are the people, and the people like them, who are up and coming who will be extremely grateful for the existence of the Nature Child.

We may wonder how we will recognise the Children who are already here, but there will be no need because the Nature Child will subconsciously realise what her position is and why she is here.

(I have now asked Spirit why they are using "she" only, rather than "he" and "she"?)

Answer: Rellman wants June to know the word "she" is used because it coincides with Mother Nature and Mother Nature is what they are trying to save.

So far, this book has been trying to make people realise the importance of saving the Planet. It cannot be stressed enough that this is imperative for our survival. It may seem unnecessary to change things now, but we must try to remember that there are many more generations to come and we need to have a safe and peaceful place for their existence.

These are our children of the future; why would we want to leave a devastated Earth as

their legacy? Realisation can be a slow dawn-
ing but one that is very necessary.

Retribution

There will be retribution, but it will not come
from the Spirit Realm. It will be Man himself
who will feel retribution for deeds done on the
Earth Realm.

Once Man understands about the need to
stop destroying the Earth Realm, then there will
be no need for retribution for what has already
been done. But if Man understands and continues to destroy the Earth, then there will be
retribution and this will come in a way that Man
will feel the wrath of what he is doing.

The Earth will become so toxic that Man will suffer the consequences. Already there have been
consequences for what has been done and there
is more to come if Man does not mend his ways.

This is where the Nature Children can help.

There are many kinds of retribution. There can be retribution for greed. There can be retribution for helping to destroy the Earth and there can be retribution for Man for being unkind and cruel. This will all be bought on by Man alone.

It is in Man's power to make a contribution, rather than causing retribution.

Measure of Sin

Sin is measured by human standards and, contrary to age-old beliefs that sin is punishable by God, the only punishment comes from Man alone.

As explained in early writings, murder, suicide and abortion are ordained deeds, so it is impossible to be punished by God or any of the other Divine that we may believe in.

Many people spend a whole lifetime in fear

of punishment by the All Mighty for deeds they have done on Earth. Their day of Judgement will come when they pass over to the Afterlife, but it will only come in the form of how much they have learnt during their incarnation on Earth. They may need to come back many more times to learn to live in peace and harmony.

(Once again, I questioned whether this information was coming from Spirit and was assured by Rellman that it was correct and to please write what is being channelled.)

The sin of the flesh is measured by Man. These are Earthly shortcomings and are not judged by the Spirit World. Some Earthly deeds have no meaning to the Spirit Realm and actions of the body are one of them.

Earth people have lived far too long under the misconception that their deeds are punishable by God and it is quite often reinforced by certain religions when going to Church.

(Rellman has allowed me to place importance on the actions of the flesh, because he wants me to know actions of the flesh merely mean pleasure of the human body. He also wants me to know pleasure of the human body places people in a very precarious position, as they believe they will be punished for certain actions.)

It is only important to humans, as this can become a Moral Ethic and humans have their own rules to live by. This is a code of ethics that we humans would hope that we could all live by.

Believe

Many people believe that the life they are now living is the only life that exists for them. They believe they are born, live their life, die and that is the end of it all.

With these writings we would like to take these people on a different journey. A journey to the wonders of what was before and one of what is after this life. For those who don't believe, we would like them to know there was much before, and there will be much after, their Earthly existence.

A Man's existence is one of many. If we can get Man to believe there are many more to come, then the Nature Child has some hope of getting Earth Plane people (the ones who believe we only have one existence) to take more care of the Planet, so it is a healthier place for them and their loved ones to come back to for the continuation of their journey.

What a wonderful thing it is to believe that when we leave this Earth it is not the end. Our bodies may die but our Spirit lives on. Our Spirit is the essence of our existence. It is what carries us through. It is the essence of the Soul and the Soul is us.

To believe is to exist and to exist is to believe.

Burdens of the Heart

Burdens of the Heart can weigh us down so much so that we cannot function properly in our daily lives. The death of a loved one can burden us heavily and a betrayal can also become a very heavy burden. It can become a burden on the Spirit and it can help destroy the Soul. We can be burdened so heavily that we begin to live in a dark place and all reason can be forsaken.

We may feel alone in our sorrow and wonder if we will ever feel normal again. Please know this is a path we have chosen to walk and it will pass.

A burden may become a burden of the Soul and a burden of the Soul can lead to depression and dark thoughts. Some of these situations are ordained and a suicide may result. This does not mean everybody who is in a dark place is meant to suicide; it only means the Souls who have chosen this will result in suicide.

Many people who spend time in a dark place can become Messengers of Spirit when they have emerged into the light. We can only become Messengers of Spirit and gain the wisdom if we have been through some dark times. Burdens of the Heart can sometimes be a very dark place. There are many other experiences, which will take us to a dark place, but know this is the only way we can gain our wisdom and become Messengers of Spirit.

Many people stay in it longer than necessary because they forget to ask Spirit for help. We can only emphasise again: Spirit is always nearby, ready and willing to help. They will only step in if we do not have the strength to carry on, but it would be so much easier to ask for help as soon as possible, to lighten the burden earlier.

Take heart and know Spirit will help us through if only we have faith and ask for help.

Mellow Angels

The title Mellow Angel is given to Earth Angels who are doing the work of Spirit on Earth. Earth Angels mean the people who have been chosen for this particular work. Many who become Earth Angels or Mellow Angels are the ones who have been through many hardships and have gained much wisdom.

Wisdom can be the most powerful weapon we can have. Wisdom can solve most problems. Wisdom can heal a heart. Wisdom can be a method of communication and passing on learnt lessons that cannot be gained any other way.

Mellow Angels possess many pearls of wisdom, which are used to benefit those who need a guiding hand. A Mellow Angel is different to the Nature Child. Mellow Angels are chosen to come to Earth and endure hardships to gain their wisdom. Nature Children are sent to Earth to begin their work as soon as they realise what they are here for.

Mellow Angels and Nature Children can both work towards the ultimate goal of healing the Earth and those on it. Mellow Angels have the gained wisdom and the Nature Children have the knowledge bought from the Spirit Realm to use for the good of Mankind.

Mellow Angels and the Nature Children have all been chosen for these particular roles and have come to Earth with open hearts to carry them out. It cannot be stressed enough the need for these chosen ones to be here. Without them, Mankind could take the Earth to destruction.

Messengers of Spirit

Messengers of Spirit are those who have been given the gift of communicating between the Earth Plane and the Spirit Realm. This is not a gift given lightly. This is a gift only given to those who will treat it with respect and who will use it how it is meant to be used.

There are many pretenders in the world and these people will only cause damage to the reputation of those who are genuinely gifted. Please choose carefully when seeking a Channel or a Medium. These Channels and Mediums are humble people and do not profess to be of greatness. A show of greatness is a sign that these people are not genuine and should be avoided at all costs.

Communication with Spirit is a very beautiful thing, both for Earth Plane people and for Spirit, for we are all as one. Messengers of Spirit go about their work quietly and are there to help in any way they can to bring comfort to those who need it or who have lost a loved one and need to know they are safe and happy.

Messengers of Spirit are dedicated people. Some have been sent to the Earth Plane with this gift because it has been earned in another lifetime and some have earned this gift here on Earth through hard work and dedication and who have gone through many experiences and hardships as ordained.

Humans have so much help and support at their disposal, if only they realised it. They have the help of the Spirit Children (The Nature Children); they have the help of the Earth Angels and they have the help of Messengers of Spirit. They can also call on Spirit and ask for help and guidance. We are never alone and will not be forsaken.

Recall the knowledge

Many people, in fleeting moments, recall some knowledge from the Spirit Realm. It may come in small flashes momentarily and it may be called "a bolt out of the blue" as humans would say.

These fleeting recollections can happen anywhere, anytime and to anybody. It may seem that we have had a brilliant insight that can help us solve a problem, but in reality it has come from the knowledge we have bought with us from the Spirit Realm. This can also happen when we look deep within for a solution.

Usually, these flashes come when we are completely unaware of anything else around us. It can come in moments of solitude when our minds are at rest. We can be unaware we are in that moment and it can sometimes be known as gazing into space when our minds drift off from Earthly things.

These moments can be the time when Spirit has the opportunity to come in and help because at these times we are connected to Spirit unbeknown to us. When our minds are cluttered with Earthly happenings there can be no connection to the Spirit Realm. This needs complete peace of mind to be able to connect to Spirit or to look within for the spiritual knowledge brought with us.

We must stress again there can be no connection to Spirit while there is constant noise and modern Man can be most at risk when he chooses to have a cluttered mind.

The Nature Children yearn for peace and quiet and will do their utmost to bring this about. Please know this is possible in time to come

❦

Memory of Going Home

───────────── ☙❧ ─────────────

There is always the memory of coming home in the back of people's mind. This is not a conscious memory, but it is there, and the ultimate goal of humans is to go home to the Spirit Realm. This unconscious memory is what drives us as humans. We are working toward the homeward journey from the time we are born, and that is the time we will be judged (we know it as Judgement Day). As mentioned before, Judgement Day is only to see how far we have come after our time on the Earth Plane.

How magnificent it would be if we could reach into our subconscious mind and recall our want to go home; then some people could make better use of their time on Earth

The reason we cannot recall the want to go home is because we come to Earth to learn lessons and this would not be possible if we had the recollections of the want to go home to the Spirit Realm.

We as Spirits must leave these words with the human population and hope for them to be able to see the errors of their ways and allow the Spirit Children to do their work to help Man to heal the Earth.

Rellman wants June to know these words come from Spirit and must be written.

Please allow yourself time to process,

absorb and accept this information.

Please know this information is true and correct.

Let these Messages be consolidated

within yourself before you move

on to the next book.

Messages From The Spirit Realm

MELLOW ANGELS

June Redfearne

Messages
from the
Spirit Realm

Rellman, Yellmean, Jeanette, Jeremy
and other Spirit Beings will relay information
through June for the book
Mellow Angels from Spirit.

Please believe this information.

Please glean this information.

**Please allow this information to be
of great help.**

Mellow Angels from Spirit

Mellow Angels from Spirit greet Spirit whenever they do their work here on Earth. Mellow Angels are called as such because they are still a few steps away from becoming Spirit Angels and they are here on Earth, sent by Spirit, to help with work to be done here on the Earth Realm.

As mentioned earlier, Mellow Angels are here to do a different job from the Nature Children. Mellow Angels have earned their position, once on Earth, by dedication and hardship. These are qualities they are sent to Earth to learn to be able to become Earth Angels and to carry out their duties. Some Mellow Angels know early their role on Earth, because they have been through enough hardships in their previous lives and have come to Earth ready to begin.

Let's not confuse these Earth Angels with the magnitude of people who are kind and generous. There are many kind and generous people on Earth and that's because they have been born with a soft heart. The Earth Angels or Mellow Angels are sent to Earth for a particular purpose and that's the difference between kind people and Earth Angels.

We will refer to these people throughout the book as Earth Angels or Mellow Angels. Please know they are one and the same.

Mellow Angels have walked many paths and, rather than be bitter about their hardships through life, they are grateful at the end of the day because they realise it has made them who they are and it could not have happened any other way. It cannot be stressed enough once again that these people are needed on Earth.

Together with the Nature Children, the Earth Angels can make a big difference to how some people live their lives. Some people only need understanding and guidance to put them on the path to where they should be and that can be where the wisdom of the Mellow Angels can do some good. If only people could understand, by raising their vibrations and rising above the actions of what goes on in the world, they then would be able to see how futile some things are and how simple it would be to clear their lives.

A way to do this is to clear their mind of earthly happenings and imagine they are sitting on a cloud overlooking the human mass. Then perhaps they could see how things could be simplified by not getting caught up in all the worry, greed, hate and trauma that some people allow in their lives.

Some of these things, such as worry and trauma, cannot be avoided, but we need to learn how not to carry the burden for too long.

Suffice to say, this clearing of the mind can be a learnt art, but to do this we must separate ourselves from worldly worries and noise and spend some time in solitude, such as meditation and relaxation, so we can reconnect with our Spiritual harmony and become a more in-tune person. We would like to remind people how close they are to Spirit and the connection is made through peace and harmony.

If there are things we do not understand, this is the time we can look to Spirit for help and guidance and this is the time Spirit can put us in touch with an Earth Angel who can be of some assistance. This is why it is very important to ask for help. Spirit will not interfere, but will wait patiently for us to ask for their help. Please know help is available.

Many people may question the validity of the connection to Spirit and at times it may seem we are being abandoned, but know we have come from Spirit so therefore we can never be abandoned. We are always connected to Spirit in our daily lives and we live with Spirit within us.

The times we may feel abandoned are the times we are left to learn a very valuable lesson, one that we have come to Earth to learn. This is only short-lived and, even during these times, we can ask for Spiritual help and guidance to get us through.

There is an endless oasis of love, knowledge and help and we are only limited by our minds, so if we can open our minds it is there for the asking. If we feel anger, hate or trauma, the Spiritual guidance is blocked off and that is why it is necessary to try to get past these feelings and to accept the help that can be offered.

It can only be said that Mellow Angels always make themselves known when the time comes that they are needed. This can come as a neighbour, a friend or a stranger, but be aware one will appear.

It may be hard to understand for some people that they may have to go through a lot of pain before their Angel appears, this is because of the wisdom we gain from the experience and this is one lesson we have come to learn.

Mellow Angels derive their name from being caring, sensitive and softly spoken people. Their only aim is to help and care for people in need. They may go about their work in an unusual way at times, but whatever they do is for the best of whomever they are trying to help.

Keeping in mind these are Angel beings, living an Earthly experience, so their way of doing things could be different to Earth Plane people, even though Earth Plane people are also Spirit beings having an Earthly experience. However, the Earth Angels are the ones chosen to do this work.

Some Earth Angels can materialise in front of our eyes and then disappear when their work is done leaving us wondering if we imagined what just happened. We are asking Earth Plane people not to expect their Earth Angel to come in any particular shape or form, meaning they can come from any walk of life and from anywhere. We must be grateful for their existence and know that they are here to help us in our times of need.

We must point out that we need to be open to this sort of intervention and not have our minds closed off to the fact that there is help available. If we close ourselves off and immerse ourselves too much in our problems, we may miss seeing the help that is there. An Earth Angel may be in front of us but, because we are shut off, we may miss the opportunity for help. Please have faith and believe.

It is a beautiful thing to have contact with our Spirit Angels whether they are Earth Angels or Angels in Spirit. We do not comprehend how much time an Angel will put into us by waiting patiently or by doing their best to contact us in some way to let us know they are there. This does not mean they will interfere, but they will do their best to let us know they are near.

We may wonder why Spirit talks about Angels rather than Guides. Guides are a very valuable connection between Man and Spirit and feature heavily in our lives as mentors and protectors.

(I now ask Rellman what is the difference between Angels and Guides)

Answer: Rellman wants June to know the difference between Angels and Guides is relatively non-existent. Celestial Beings are all there to help and guide us on our journey through life. Where we might call a very kind and helpful human an Angel, it is the same for Spirit Beings. A Guide can also be referred to as an Angel.

Some Spirit Beings are more advanced than others and the appropriate one will appear or put us in touch with an Earth Angel for what our needs are at the time.

Mellow Angels continually make themselves available to their human counterparts, knowing it is their calling and they are doing their work at the request of the Spirit Angels. Help can also come directly from Spirit and please know this is available for the asking. It is so important to believe this is possible.

We ask that humans be mindful of not abusing the Spirit intervention. In other words, we ask that people do not want or expect divine intervention if their purpose is not pure, such as wanting harm to come to another person. By doing this we are setting ourselves back in our purpose on Earth. Spirit does not take kindly to this sort of request.

The Quest for Peace and Harmony

———— ❧ ————

Every Man has within him the power for peace, so why then does peace not reign on Earth? It is simply because Man has lessons to learn, but he does not realise that these lessons can be achieved and he can still have peace in his heart.

We want to teach people that they are on Earth to learn and to gain wisdom and sometimes these lessons can be very hard. If only Earth Plane people would keep in mind that these lessons are not punishments but rewards gained in a very hard way, then perhaps Man could keep peace in his heart, knowing the gift of knowledge he would receive at the end of it.

There is a misconception that God punishes people for deeds done on Earth, but we want them to know that this is not possible, because Man is sent to Earth to learn and, unless he makes mistakes and goes through hardships, he does not gain the wisdom. Therefore, it is impossible for God to punish something that is Man's journey on Earth.

We must remind Man that deeds such as murder and suicide are ordained deeds so cannot, and are not, punishable by God. We ask: "Why would God want to punish someone for ordained deeds or deeds done in ignorance that could cause harm to others?" It is Man's lesson to learn not to cause harm to others and sometimes this can only be learnt by making mistakes.

Natural Disasters and Wars

We may wonder how we can keep peace when there are so many disasters and wars happening in the world? Once again, these events are ordained. The people who are killed by these incidents have asked for this to happen to them before they left the Spirit

World. We each choose how and when we will leave the Earth Plane. People can choose to die by war because until there is peace on Earth, war will continue. Once Man can have peace in his heart and love for his fellow Man, there will be no more wars.

Natural disasters, as we know them, are not always natural. They can sometimes be caused by Man's interference with the environment. This is why it is imperative for Man to stop what he is doing and begin to heal the Earth.

Cause and Effect

What Man causes has a huge effect on life on the Earth and those on it. The main cause is Man's inability to understand what damage is being done and the effect it will have on Mankind. We as Spirit only want what is best for Man and, even though he can have some monumental ordeals to go through at times, Spirit is always there to help and guide Man on his way.

There is absolutely no reason to be destroying the Earth. There is plenty for everyone if only Man could be a little less greedy and think more about his fellow humans and the generations to come.

There is more cause and effect than Earth Plane people can imagine. Every time Man causes some damage, there is an effect to follow. It has some effect on the Earth and it affects everyone on it.

Poor People from Spirit

People who are poor on this Earth have chosen to be this way, so they can live a humble life and experience what comes with it. These people may have lived an affluent life previously, but they now want to know what it is like to be poor. We do not consciously know we have chosen this, because it was decided before we left the Spirit Realm.

There are many things that can be learnt from a poor experience. One lesson can be humility, by living beneath the level of more prosperous people. One is of strength to be able to cope and survive with very little to live on. Another is to learn we are equally valuable people and loved equally as much by Spirit as our richer counterparts.

Living poor is a very valuable experience and should not be perceived as a punishment. Some of the greatest people, who have lived on Earth through the ages, have been poor. Being poor is also an opportunity to be able to ask for help from the Spirit World and our Earth Angels.

This does not mean Spirit can make us rich or solve all our problems, but by asking for help it can ease the burden and make life more pleasant, which in turn can clear the mind enough to find a solution to our problems in our daily lives.

An Angel may sit on our shoulder and tap away at our consciousness in the hope we may hear them to let us know they are around. Please open your heart and let them in.

Fellow Angels and Fellow People

———— ❧◈❧ ————

Fellow Angels and Fellow People work side by side every day even though most people are unaware this is happening.

(I have now asked Rellman to explain what is meant by Fellow Angels and Fellow People, as sometimes things can be channelled in an unusual way. Why they have used these terms is a mystery to me, but as I am the Spirit Messenger and not the author, I oblige.)

Explanation: Rellman wants June to know Fellow Angels are the Earth Angels and Fellow People are the Earth Plane people.

Every time Earth Plane people feel a miracle has occurred no matter how small, it is the Spirit Angels doing their work, because we have subconsciously asked for or wanted help. Every time we feel someone has done us a great service on Earth, it is the Earth Angels doing their work.

How many times has this sort of thing happened to us and we dismiss it as just being lucky, or being in the right place at the right time? This is not a coincidence or a stroke of luck and this is why it is imperative for the Earth Plane people to understand how this happens, so they know they can have faith that there is help available.

Please just ask.

Bird Angels

We want to mention the magnificent birds. Birds are Angels on wings. Birds can bring happiness to almost anyone with their beautiful free spirit and their angelic song.

Birds are an essential part of life and nature and, if Man is not careful, birds could be a casualty of Man's destruction and greed. Birds can often bring messages of hope to our sullied Soul;

we only need to be in nature and listen to a bird sing and it can bring healing to a heavy heart.

These beautiful creatures are messengers from Spirit; messengers of hope and happiness and can uplift the Soul. Birds and animals are an integral part of our existence and we need Man to stop destroying what is his hope for the future.

Where Do We Come From?

We come from the space of infinity, where there is no beginning and where there is no end. Man begins a journey from whence we cannot comprehend and Man continues his journey to where there is no end.

Man's journey is an ongoing path to Eternal Glory and, when reached, it is then an Eternal existence in Paradise.

This may explain in part why Man's journey can sometimes seem very difficult. It is through these difficulties and experiences that Man learns and grows and puts him on the path to Eternal Salvation.

Spirit wants Man to know when things seem impossible and life is hard, then that is when Man is on his journey to Glory.

Reaching the Other Side

When reaching the other side after our journey from the Earth Plane to the Spirit Realm, we still have with us all our energies and personalities that we had on the Earth Plane. It is almost as though we had never left. However, some of the energies and memories feel very strange once we have reached the Spirit Realm. This is because a lot of the energies are from experiences we have had on the Earth Plane and are no longer relevant in the Spirit World.

An instance of this could be: if a human being felt anger or hate towards another Earth Being, then these energies are neither warranted nor beneficial in the Afterlife. When we first arrive, it takes some time for these feelings to dissolve, which at times can be quite confusing, as we feel we are still in human form. However, there is so much help from our Spirit Beings and our family and friends, who have passed before, that it makes the transition a lot smoother.

Suffice to say: this may take some time to adjust to before we realise we have passed over into the Spirit Realm. It is comforting to know, even though we may be going through a confusing time, that there is always help and guidance at all times and that we are perfectly safe.

We may wonder, however, how our energies stay around those we love on Earth and are also with us when we arrive in the Spirit Realm. It is the negative energies we bring with us that will dissolve and, because they have been with us for some time on the Earth Plane, it can become confusing when they start to disappear once in the Hereafter.

Rellman wants June to know energies transcend from the Earth Plane to the Spirit Realm. Energies are like Mercury, so that they can be left behind and also carried to the Spirit Realm.

It can be a very jubilant experience once we

realise where we are, because of all the wonderful family and friends around us, whom we have not seen for a very long time. It can be a celebration of life after life with the ones we have missed for so long.

There comes a time when we feel the loss of the ones we left behind, but it is very comforting to know we will all be reunited in time to come. We can also contact the ones left behind by trying to let them know we are still around and not lost to them.

This can also be done in reverse. Earth Plane people can contact their passed over loved ones by talking to them while keeping an open mind and heart and looking and listening for signs of contact. Know that passed over loved ones will be trying to contact them in due course.

Note: These next four chapters and others through the rest of the book have been channelled by a new Spirit Entity by the name of Plellal, who has come through specifically to talk about crippled children. It took me some time to realise that a new Spirit was present, but once I realised what was happening it became a very pleasant experience.

Crippled Children

ꙮ

Plellal from Spirit wants Earth Plane people to know that crippled children come to Earth with a desire either to be born crippled, or to become crippled later in childhood.

These beautiful Souls have chosen this before leaving the Spirit World, and it is their way of learning a very valuable lesson, both for themselves and those around them. These children believe they can both teach to, and learn from, the mainstream human race about compassion and love.

These children can sometimes test the patience of those around them and it is then that the crippled children can teach these people some tolerance and patience. On the other hand, these children are here to learn that some people are not always loving and caring.

The people who care for these children have also chosen this path before leaving the Spirit World. It is a contract between the Souls before descending to Earth. Once on Earth it is unknown to the parties that this was ordained until they once again reach the Spirit Realm. Subconsciously, the lesson of loving, caring and patience is being learnt.

These children can be physically crippled, but they can also be emotionally, mentally or spiritually crippled. Whatever the affliction, they have come to Earth to experience this specific lesson for themselves and for those who care for them.

We as humans must live with human emotions and this burden can become quite tiresome, but let it be known that Spirit does not give us any more than we can handle and it takes very special people to have chosen this path.

The Day We Are Born

The day we are born is the day we are set on our path to glory. This is one lifetime of many, some from before and some to come.

Each lifetime is a step closer to our ultimate goal of peace and eternal glory.

Some people have many more lifetimes to live and some are close to their final destination. Spirit smiles on those who accept their path with joy in their hearts no matter what we have chosen for ourselves.

Unless we know, or learn, how Spirit works, it could be very difficult to have joy in our hearts when life can be very traumatic at times. That is why it is important for these books to be written so people can understand how we choose the path we do when we come to Earth. Knowing this, it may be a lot easier to accept, especially because of the knowledge and wisdom we gain and knowing it is taking us to our ultimate goal... taking us home to the Spirit Realm.

Please understand, even when life is traumatic, there are some very beautiful experiences to be had and these are the things we must concentrate on.

Abandonment

⊱❦⊰

This word can have many meanings. Some people are abandoned at birth; some are abandoned during life and some just feel abandoned.

If we are abandoned at birth, we have particularly chosen this path for ourselves as there are many and varied lessons to be learnt through this. If we are abandoned later in life, this is also a choice we have made before coming to Earth, so therefore we create circumstances that will lead to abandonment by others.

When we just feel abandoned there may be no justification for feeling this way. It may be a negative point of view and really have no substance for this feeling. Some people may project the image of being abandoned in the hope that it will make others take note and feel sorry for them.

In other cases, a feeling of abandonment can be a short-lived experience and this may happen because of some emotional setback in our lives or we may feel at this time that no one cares. This abandonment feeling is lifted once the crisis is over. Other times, when we feel abandoned and there is no evidence of why this should be, it is because the person has chosen their life to end in suicide and this is the first step towards it.

Abandonment also has another meaning: one where a person may choose to abandon another. There are many reasons for this also. One is where a selfish person may feel the responsibility of another is interfering with their lifestyle and may choose to abandon the unwanted person.

If we have chosen this life for ourselves before coming to Earth, we may choose parents and friends who will abide by our choice unwittingly, and abandon us.

Abandonment can weaken our resolve, or it can make us stronger and, no matter how we feel, we must have faith that there are Spirit Angels and Earth Angels there to help, so please ask.

Retaliation

———————— ⸎ ————————

Many circumstances that occur in our lives may make us feel as though we need to retaliate against any wrongs we think are being done, or have been done to us.

It has been an automatic reaction in the past to retaliate when we feel threatened or damaged. This has been an instinctive survival mechanism, but Man has come a long way since the cave days and it is no longer in their best interest to react this way.

Blessed is the Man who can turn the other cheek. Blessed is the Man who can love and forgive under extreme circumstances. Blessed is the Man who can stand tall in the face of adversity and blessed is the Man who can give a helping hand to those who may abuse us.

Retaliation has no place in the service of Man or God and those who continue to use this method will find no peace. They may find a short-lived satisfaction, but in the long run it will give them no peace and peace is what every Man needs to strive for.

Retaliation can have a domino effect in a negative way, whilst love and forgiveness can have a domino effect in a positive way.

Plentiful

Man has yet to realise that all resources on Earth are plentiful. He also has to realise that there is enough for everyone if only Man could learn to share with his less fortunate counterparts.

It may seem in some areas that there is not enough food and shelter to go around, but there are also people who have way too much and could easily share this around. This brings it back to Man's greed and unwillingness to give.

As it has been written before, many people on Earth who are poor have chosen this life for themselves, while many people have chosen to come back and experience an affluent lifestyle. In each case there is a huge lesson to be learnt. The many people who are poor and the many people who are affluent have made a contract before leaving the Spirit Realm, each coming to Earth to learn a very valuable lesson from the other.

The poor people learn that the affluent people are not always kind and generous to their poorer counterparts and by this the poor person learns that it is better to be poor and generous of heart than to be greedy and rich. The rich people are here to learn that by giving to the less fortunate people, their hearts can be filled with happiness and peace. Each lesson brings them closer to their ultimate goal of eternal salvation.

There are still many more poor people on Earth who have chosen this way of life and who will be poor all their lives. These people are here to learn a different lesson. There are also many more affluent people on Earth who will be this way all their lives and they are also here to learn a different lesson from the group above.

Rich or poor, we all have the capabilities for kindness and generosity, but many people choose not to be so and may have to come back many more times until the lesson is learnt.

❤

Subconscious

⸻ ❧ ⸻

Everybody who comes to Earth has a subconscious job or way of life they have chosen for themselves. We say subconscious because we are not aware of this once we enter the Earth Plane and, only when we return to the Spirit World, do we acknowledge and remember this choice.

Spirit wants Earth Plane people to understand this procedure and hopefully accept the life they have chosen for themselves. It may seem unlikely that we would burden ourselves with a certain way of life, which could be very hard and traumatic at times, but if we are aware that this is so and we can accept this fact, then life on Earth could be easier to bear.

This is especially so, knowing the rewards it

will bring on Judgement Day and beyond and how much closer we are to our journey's end, which will take us to the Spirit World and eternal peace and glory.

Misjudging

How many times has a person misjudged another? We mostly make a judgement immediately we encounter another human being. Maybe this person is overweight and, because of this, we instantly think they are greedy and eat too much. We may encounter someone who is dishevelled and unkempt and we immediately think they are lazy and up to no good.

We also make judgements from another point of view. We automatically presume someone who is well dressed and neat and tidy is a good person and a pillar of society. These may be small presumptions but we begin to build a point of view of these people and may treat them accordingly.

Spirit wants Man to know we cannot all be the same and we are all here for different purposes. We are all at different stages of our development and we are all here to learn and grow. We are also here to learn tolerance and kindness towards other human beings.

Let the overweight Man and the unkempt Man shine in the glory of God and let the neat and tidy Man understand we are all equal in the eyes of the universe. Let us be kind to our fellow Man and extend a helping hand and save our judgement, for we will be judged.

There is always a reason for people being the way they are. They come to Earth with a specific purpose and live their lives accordingly to create what they have come to learn and if that's being overweight or unkempt so be it. We must allow these people their peace to live how they have chosen to live and allow them to learn the lessons and gain the wisdom they have come for.

Jubilation

Jubilation is when we return to the Spirit Realm. Jubilation and glory is when we meet friends and loved ones who have passed before. Jubilation and celebration is for all those we have missed for so long and for those who have recently passed. It is a celebration of togetherness with those we love and it is a celebration of being back home in the Spirit Realm.

What a wonderful coming home when we can see what our journey was all about during our incarnation on the Earth Plane. How clear it all becomes and how wonderful it is to be free of all worries and burdens of our life on Earth. We can rejoice in our achievements; see the error of our ways; and we realise that this had to be so, so that we could develop and grow.

Spirit can only hope that by reading these books, we learn that this is our journey and hopefully we can embrace it as part of our destiny.

Teachings

ﬁ⁓∾⁓

Can we be taught anything, or do we need to learn the lessons by ourselves? In some cases, we can be taught some things and in other cases we need to learn by ourselves. This is where the Earth Angels can come in by imparting some of their knowledge on to whoever may need it. Earth Angels can put us on the right path with their insightfulness and wisdom. Having said this, it is only a guideline and we do have to make decisions for ourselves. No matter what help we get, our lives are mapped out and, by this it means, we must learn by our mistakes.

Earth Angels and Spirit Angels can help in many ways. They can lighten our burden when we ask for help and they can try to guide us as much as possible, but we still must learn the lessons we came to Earth to learn.

We may always think that by teachings, it means someone will teach us what to do, but in reality it is the earthly experiences we have in the most part that are doing the teaching.

What if we never had a problem? We would never learn to cope with one. What if we never had any painful experiences? We would never know what to do if we needed to help someone else who had had a painful experience. What if we never had any other hard dealings with life? Our lives would become mute and there would be no need for us to be here.

Pain, hardships and mistakes are the teachings of life, but please remember Earth Angels and Spirit Angels are always around to lighten our load.

Bless our hardships and our mistakes for that is who we are.

Channelling

To be able to channel we need to be considerably advanced in our journey back to the Spirit World. Our capability to channel has come from many lifetime experiences. The closer we are to our return home to the Spirit Realm for the last time, the easier it is for us to be able to connect to the afterlife by channelling.

Channelling means we have open communication between Earth and the Spirit World. We must therefore use this for the good of Mankind. For some people they may never be able to hear Spirit talking to them and this is where a Channel can step in and help with communication between the two worlds.

A Channel therefore must be pure of heart, for there must never be any malice in the messages between the two realms. A true Channel has only one aim and that is to help his fellow Man by imparting a very important message from the other side, which will be very beneficial to the person concerned.

This is one example of an Earth Angel appearing when needed, for Channels are Earth Angels. We must, however be wary of those who portray themselves as Channels and therefore create more discord in the life of an unsuspecting person.

Please choose wisely when wanting a message

from the other side and make sure the Channel you have chosen is of the purest form.

Broken Spirits

We would like to point out that it is not the actual Spirit that is broken, but it is our resolve that has been broken. This may happen when so many hardships and traumas occur in our life and it has become increasingly hard to cope with the burden.

We must go back to the information about suicide. This may be one reason we have allowed our resolve to be broken, knowing sub-consciously we have chosen suicide as our way of leaving the Earth Plane.

Not all cases of broken resolve are meant to end in suicide. A human may feel he has exhausted all avenues of help to get him back on track to live a healthy life, but there is still one option he may not have exercised and that is the help of the

Earth Angels and the Spirit Angels, who are all waiting and ready for when their help is needed.

Man may allow himself to be broken of resolve because he does not realise that there is so much help available and how much strength Man possesses, if only he chooses to use it.

How many times has Man been down and the only way he can see out is to look to the Universe, God and the Angels for help? This is also one way of getting some people to realise that help is available and, by learning this, they can then go ahead and teach other people the importance of asking for Spiritual guidance. These people can also become Earth Angels by going through these traumatic hardships.

Forgiveness

How many times has a disservice been done to us and we are not able to forgive the perpetrator? This can be one of the hardest things to do in life, to forgive someone who has harmed us in some way.

At times, the perpetrator may carry the burden of this and ask for our forgiveness. Other times they may be completely detached from what they have done and this is when it becomes extremely difficult for some people to be able to forgive them.

We must realise this is also a lesson we have come to learn. The perpetrator has been commissioned in our lives to carry out the harm he has laid upon us and it is now our lesson to learn to forgive.

It may become a heavy load for us to carry, if we do not learn to forgive, for it can fester inside of us and in the end we realise we are the only person it is hurting. We can carry hate and resentment, which can interfere with our lives, while the perpetrator may go on and be seemingly unaware of the harm he has caused.

We must free ourselves of hate and resentment and allow our Spirit to soar in the knowledge that we have forgiven and can carry on with our lives free of that heavy burden.

Chosen Parents

―――――――――― ❧❧ ――――――――――

Before we descend to Earth we choose who our parents are going to be. As written before, we come to Earth to learn and grow and, because of this, we need to choose parents who will help teach us some of these lessons.

We sometimes may wonder why our lives are not going the way we want them to go and why our parents are the way they are. This could be because the parents we have chosen are poor people and we would prefer to live a more affluent lifestyle. It may be that our parents are being hard with discipline or that they may abandon us. Whatever the case, all these experiences are teaching the lessons we have come to learn. They are making us strong and resilient for whatever our chosen role is in this life.

These learnings can be the beginning of us becoming Earth Angels, Healers or Teachers and this is the reason for choosing these people as our parents. Some people are only together long enough to conceive our beautiful Souls and we must accept the fact that if one of these people has gone out of our lives, they were only meant to be there so we could be bought into this world to live and learn and to do the job we were meant to do.

There are so many circumstances for why and how we are born and who our parents are, but know none of this is by chance. We hope by knowing this, we are more able to accept our circumstances, for this is what we have chosen for ourselves.

Knowing Ourselves

It can be one of the most important things for us to know ourselves. This is why it is imperative to have the information written in these books so that we know where we come from and why we are here.

Once this knowledge is known, we may be more accepting of our circumstances and begin to learn and grow from this.

Knowing our reason for being here can clear up any confusion and allow us the freedom to make our journey much more pleasant, without spending so much time on the whys and wherefores of our existence.

So much time is spent on people wondering why has this happened to me, why was I born this way and why am I not as fortunate as some other people? We must all remember we are extremely fortunate, no matter what the circumstances. We are all Spiritual creatures, all equally important in the eyes of the Universe and we all eventually come home to the Spirit World, where we shall all live in eternal peace.

We ask that no matter how hard life may seem, it is important to make the most of this incarnation and value the growth and wisdom we gain from it.

Knowledge is power and through this we can empower our lives. From the beginning to the end our journey is a learning experience. Please embrace this and know the Angels are there to help.

Perseverance

The magic word is perseverance. Perseverance can come from knowledge; knowledge is power and power is what we need to persevere.

How many times have we found that if we persevere everything turns out for the best? How many times have we decided to give up before the end and realise, had we persevered, we would have succeeded?

Giving up is time lost that can never be regained. That time lost could have been the element to our success. Success does not necessarily mean wealth and possessions. Success can mean every little advancement we make in our daily lives.

Man does not realise how much power and endurance he has until he is tested and it is only then that, if he chooses to use it, he will succeed.

Perseverance can be the means of the first tiny step; Perseverance can be the means of learning to love and forgive; Perseverance can be any little step we make to better our lives.

Spirit perseveres with us as humans. Spirit never gives up on any one of us. Spirit is always there to help no matter what we choose to do with our lives. Spirit perseveres with love and tolerance and hopefully we can do the same.

Obligations

Obligations can mean many things. We may feel obligated to do something for someone else that we know is not right and we may not want to do it. If we carry out this service we may be putting ourselves back in our journey in life.

When we feel obligated to do something for someone else that may not feel right, we are putting our own desires on hold to oblige someone else. This does not hold us in good stead for our own development.

If we feel we would like to do a good service and lend a helping hand to someone else, out of the kindness of our heart, then this will be a wonderful opportunity for our own advancement in life.

We do have obligations in life, however, firstly to ourselves and then to our fellow Man. Our obligation is to live as good a life as possible and to give a helping hand to anyone who may need it.

Our obligation is to be aware of the reason we are here and be grateful every day for the experience. Our obligation is to love and care for each other and to forgive any wrongs done to us. Our obligation is not to destroy the Earth, or to be greedy, cruel and selfish to each other. Our obligation is not to have obligations that will take us on the wrong path, but to let our Spirit be free for now and always.

Blessings

Spirit wants Man to know how very blessed we are to have the opportunity of this lifetime as another step towards salvation.

How blessed we are to have the people we

have in our lives and how blessed we are to live on this beautiful Earth for the time we are here. We want Man to understand and appreciate the beauty of the Earth and to stop destroying it as though it is his right to do so.

We will find blessings every day if we care to look for them and how blessed we are to have the Spirit Angels forever supporting and loving us in our time of need.

Please allow yourself time to process,

absorb and accept this information.

Please know this information is true and correct.

Let these Messages be consolidated
within yourself

before you move on to the next book.

Messages From
The Spirit Realm

LIFE AND THE AFTER LIFE

June Redfearne

Messages
from the
Spirit Realm
Life and the Afterlife

Rellman, Yellmean, Jeanette, Jeremy, Yellow Feathers, Plellal, Reokmank, and other Spirit Beings will relay information through June.

Please believe this information.

Please glean this information.

Please allow this information to be of great help.

Life and the Afterlife

――――――――― ❧❧ ―――――――――

ife and the Afterlife is a comprehensive coverage of life, both here on Earth and in the Spirit World. Many of these subjects have already been covered in the previous three books and hopefully many messages have been comprehended by reading these books.

We want Man to understand his reason for being on the Earth Plane and to bring some clarification to his life, as it may be hard to comprehend the whys and wherefores of life and why we are here. As explained in previous writings, Man comes to Earth to go on a journey of living and learning, to gain insight and wisdom which will take him back home to the Spirit Realm and on the path to Eternal Glory.

From the day we are born to the day we return to the Spirit Realm, regardless of what lifetime we are living, and how many lifetimes we have already lived, the journey is comprehensive and educational. No matter what we would prefer our lives to be, we will all go on the journey we have chosen for ourselves to learn the specific lessons we have come to learn.

We have already learnt in previous writing ways in which we can make our existence on the Earth Plane easier for ourselves by looking to our homeland, the Spirit Realm, for comfort whenever we need it. The Spirit Realm is like a Mother comforter and Man is like the newborn child. Whereas a human child can look to its Mother for comfort, so can Man look to the Spirit World for comfort and support.

We are never alone. Man can sometimes feel abandoned in his Earthly life, but he will always be taken care of from the Spirit Realm.

We have already learnt our main purpose for being on the Earth Plane. Let the love of God shine; fear not for we are safe.

Man is told constantly that he is safe, yet he questions the validity of this statement when so many traumatic things can happen to us in our lifetime, such as murder, starvation, war, degradation and many more. Our human experiences may not always keep our bodies safe, but our Soul and our Spirit is always safe. No matter what happens to us on the Earth Plane, our Soul will always reach the Afterlife safe and secure.

Our Soul is us. Our body is a carriage in which

we exist whilst on the Earth Plane. Our bodies are disposable and dispensable, but our Soul lives on in the eternal light of God and the Afterlife.

May the light eternally shine upon us. May the love of God or the Universe be eternally with us, and may our journey be filled with wonder and awe, until we come home and bask in Eternal Glory.

For the love of God and Man himself, let us continue our journey with wisdom, patience and love. If we do not have wisdom, let us earn it. If we do not have patience, let us earn that as well and if we do not have love, let the love of God and kindness shine through us and hold us in good stead.

Man manifests himself through his thoughts and actions to arrive at a place where he can learn the most. In other words, if Man has come to Earth to learn a specific lesson, then he will subconsciously manifest that situation in his life so that he can learn that lesson. That is why it is imperative for us as human beings to allow people to be where they are in life and not to judge or be critical, for we too are at our own learning stage.

We have learnt so many valuable lessons over time, but none as important as learning to love each other. Love is the most valuable emotion of all emotions. Love is the Teacher, the Healer, the Giver and the Doer. Love extends all boundaries and we must learn to love the Soul, not the body, and all else will fade away.

How the Soul Exists

We may wonder how the Soul lives on in the Afterlife when the body is buried in the ground. For those who don't already know, the Soul leaves the body at the moment of death of the human carriage in which it exists. The Spirit carries the Soul to the Afterlife and it is then the Spirit is free to be wherever it needs to be and that is sometimes around those we have left behind. The Spirit, as explained before, is like energy and that energy is like mercury and can be anywhere it needs to be.

The amount of time our Soul spends in the Afterlife before being reincarnated into another life of learning on Earth can be long or short. This will depend on how soon the Soul wants to learn everything it needs to know and how soon it wants to exist in Eternal Glory.

The complexity of it all can be explained in the simplest way: We come to Earth to live and learn, we leave, and when the time is right we exist in the Hereafter in Eternal Glory.

Time to Heal

Some Souls need time to heal from a traumatic life on Earth, or one of sickness. In these cases the Soul will spend more time being healed and preparing for its next journey to Earth. It may also need to wait for the appropriate body in which to exist whilst on the Earth Plane, so it can learn the lesson it needs to learn.

We need to be born to the people who are going to live the life that is going to teach us the most on this journey. They exist in the circumstances that we need and once born we also help create what we need to learn.

Many Souls prefer to stay in the Afterlife for a longer period because they recall the traumatic time they went through whilst on the Earth Plane. After such a time the Soul can be a little hesitant to go back again soon after and, as explained before, the circumstances need to be right.

When a Soul is ready to reincarnate, the Spirit will bring the Soul to Earth to be born to whomever it has chosen to be born to. The Spirit stays with the Soul until it is once again ready to leave the body and return to the Afterlife.

The Soul can remember everything up to the point of being born and then the memories of its previous life or lives cannot be recalled. However, some small children do have some sort of recollection of their previous life for a short time and some can remember briefly who they were. All this information is locked away in our subconscious and, in extreme circumstances, some of it can be recalled. Information about previous lives can be recalled under hypnosis, or if some event triggers a memory, but it is rare to be able to recall information from the Afterlife.

Trauma of the Soul

When a Soul comes to Earth to learn what it needs to learn, in an incarnation where it exists in a body that has come to carry out a contract with another Soul, it can sometimes become traumatised because of the life it has chosen to live within the human body.

This particular human may be on Earth to carry out some heinous crime against another human and this is where the contract between the two Souls comes in. The perpetrator and the victim have chosen this life, so as to learn as much as possible in this situation whilst on Earth.

The Soul has prepared itself for this kind of existence and, because the Soul is pure, it would normally be against any of these actions, but it knows it has to live this particular life to learn what it needs to learn.

When the Soul has been traumatised in this way it sometimes needs longer in the Afterlife to recover before it chooses to come back to Earth for another lifetime of learning. The Soul may also choose to come back as soon as possible to do what it needs to do and therefore reach Eternal Glory sooner.

⚘

Ascending Soul

⸎

The ascending Soul prepares itself to leave the body at the time of death. It has known for some time when death will occur as this has been chosen by the Soul before re-entering the Earth Plane. We say the ascending Soul because it is ready to be taken by the Spirit and ascend to the Afterlife.

In a case where the body has been really sick and it is ready to expire, the Soul has stopped functioning within that body sometime before the actual death. It has prepared itself to leave the moment the body expires.

In the case of a sudden death such as a car accident, the Soul knows the impact is coming but it can still be a little traumatised by the event. This is also the case if the person is murdered, the Soul can also be a little traumatised until the act has finished and the body expires.

In some cases of murder or traumatic death, the Soul will leave the body before death occurs, so as to prevent the body suffering more than is bearable. If there is no Soul then the body becomes lifeless even though the organs are functioning for the time being.

We must take heart that Spirit will not allow us to suffer any more than we can bear. It is surprising what a Human can endure and will in extreme cases, but at the point of being unbearable, the Soul will leave the body and go on to the Afterlife.

The Closeness of the Afterlife

Many of us on the Earth Plane feel the Afterlife is many hundreds of miles in the yonder, above the Earth, but in actual fact the Afterlife can be as close as a few feet away from where we are. Our human capabilities do not allow us to see into the next dimension where the Soul exists, until the Soul is ready for another Earth journey. When we know this, it makes it more easily understood how the Spirit can stay around us and also take the Soul to and from the Afterlife. The Afterlife can be closer to us than our bodies are once they are buried in the Earth.

Spirit wants people to understand this so they realise their loved ones are not lost to them. Spirit also encourages people to talk to their loved ones, as they are closer than we imagine and this is why we can feel their presence at times because of their close proximity to where we are.

The time when we may feel as though we can

glimpse a departed loved one around us is the time when our human capabilities are able to see into the next dimension. This is usually only short-lived and the majority of humans do not have this capability. This is also the reason our loved ones can visit us in our sleep at times, because their dimension is so close to ours it makes it possible for them to come to us when we are in a relaxed state.

Our departed loved ones are around us all the time. They can see us because they are in a place of higher consciousness than we are and there is only a thin veil between us and the Afterlife, or the "Spirit world", as humans may call it. This thin veil can be crossed when the circumstances are right, such as when we are in a deeply relaxed state of mind or when we are asleep.

Spirit must stress that our departed loved ones are very close, so close in actual fact that they are not gone, it is just that we cannot see them. We co-exist with the Afterlife every day and it is comforting to know how close it is to us.

Our fellow Angel Souls talk to us, walk with us and are with us at all times. They do their utmost to let us know that they are near. The only barrier

to connecting to them is our grief or our ignorance of the fact that our Dear Ones are so close.

Signs from the Other Side

When our loved ones, or our loved animals,
pass over to the other side, we quite often
feel that this is the last we will see or feel them.
Spirit wants us to know this is not the end; it is
only the end of a chapter for the passed over
loved one.

As humans, we need to feel some sort of closeness to our departed family or friend. If we can't
feel their energy around us then we need some
other sign that they still exist and are close to us.
This is when our departed loved ones can show
us some sign that they are still near.

To do this they may allow us to smell a familiar scent belonging to the departed person.
This can come in the form of a perfume that the

person used to wear, the smell of the tobacco the person used to smoke, or any other familiar smell associated with that person.

Another way we can see signs is that of an insect, a butterfly, or bird, when we think of that person. A butterfly may land on our shoulder at the time when we are thinking about our loved one, or a bird may come close and stay around longer to show us this is a sign our departed loved one is still around us.

They can show us in many ways that they are still around us and watching over us. Please, be at peace and know that they will never forsake us and will always try to contact us in some way.

Lost Souls

A Soul that doesn't pass over completely for some reason will exist between the two dimensions, until it eventually passes or has help to pass. It can sometimes get lost in the transition, mainly because the Spirit is not strong enough to complete the journey of taking the Soul to the Afterlife. The Soul can remain lost for a very long time unless it gets help to complete the journey.

The Soul can become disorientated and it is not sure which way to go. We humans can sometimes sense there is a lost Soul around us and it is then we can help it by encouraging it to go home to the Afterlife. We can encourage it to go to the light. (This is a human saying to describe the Afterlife.) Some people are capable of channelling an entity (lost Soul) through them and that is when this Soul can be urged to move on to the next dimension. It is then that one of the Soul's loved ones who have passed before will come for it. This can be easily achieved because of the closeness of the Other Side.

Even though a Soul can get lost, it can exist and endure until it finds its rightful place again. This is why it is said the Soul is always safe. Even though the Spirit has not completed the job of taking the Soul to the Afterlife, the Spirit returns to Earth to be around the loved ones the departed Soul has left behind. The Spirit will gather momentum whilst on the Earth Plane, so it is ready to bring the previously lost Soul back to Earth when it is ready to begin another journey.

For many Souls that become lost it can be an extremely difficult time, but it can also be one of great learning and experience. This may even take it closer to Eternal Glory in a shorter time than if it had not been lost. This is because of the wisdom it has gained from being a lost Soul.

When a Soul Returns

When the Soul returns to Earth to begin another journey, it brings with it refreshed and renewed vitality to hold it in good stead for its next lifetime on the Earth Plane. It needs an abundance of energy to cope with the birth of its human body.

If the foetus is meant to be aborted or mis-carried, the Soul will need the energy to leave the body so soon to return to the Afterlife and, if the human body is stillborn, the Soul also needs extra energy to leave the body and return to the Afterlife.

The Spirit takes the Soul to and from the Afterlife, but energy is still needed by the Soul to do the return trip so soon. This is especially so when a Soul is born as a crippled or sick child. When a child is born with some disability, it is noticed how much fighting strength this child will have and that is because of the energy of the Soul.

The Soul detaches itself emotionally from any trauma or problems the new child is born with. In other words the Soul has chosen this path and it has accepted whatever may come along with this new life it is about to lead. It also does not become traumatised over having to go back to the Afterlife so soon after abortion or miscarriage, for that is also what it has chosen. The lesson has been learnt and it is free to go back home until its next chosen journey.

When Souls Meet

We may wonder why it is that when we meet someone that they seem very familiar. This is because these Souls have had past life connections and are meeting up in this life to resolve unfinished business or continue their lives together.

Some Souls have come to atone for wrongs done to another in a previous life. Some have come to reconnect with loved ones and continue their journey together. Some Souls reconnect with loved ones over and over, different bodies, different circumstances, but same Soul connection. Whichever the case, there is always a valuable lesson to be learnt.

When Souls come together, they recognise each other immediately and that is why we sometimes feel we know somebody we have never met before and this is why we feel comfortable with certain people when we haven't known them for very long.

Sometimes the roles can be reversed in this

life. For instance a man may choose to live a life as a woman, or a woman may choose to live a life as a man and these two previously known Souls may marry and learn what it is like living as the opposite sex. Each and every situation is a learning experience.

In other cases, sisters and brothers may become sons and daughters and various other connections can be made in this manner. Our worst enemy may come back to become our best friend and atone for wrongs done in a previous life. Whatever the case, all parties realise they need to learn the lesson of this new life.

No matter what we do or how we live, the Soul is always pure.

Time of Resolution

When we pass over to the other side, we meet up with family, friends and other people we have known on the Earth Plane and who have passed earlier. Many issues can be resolved between people that occurred on the Earth Plane and it can be decided to come back to Earth to co-exist with each other to continue a life of resolution.

Some conflicts cannot be resolved in one lifetime, although in our existence we may not realise that this conflict has spanned across several lifetimes. The lesson we are learning here is how to co-exist peacefully so there is no more conflict.

We may meet someone we take an instant dislike to for no apparent reason. This is because there has been no resolution in earlier existences. When we understand this, we can make some effort to make peace with this person. We can do this by befriending them and doing our best to co-exist with them in a peaceful manner.

Twin Souls

Twin Souls are where two Souls keep living through several lifetimes as companions. They choose to come to Earth and reincarnate in twin babies, where they live in harmony for their Earthly existence. If the Souls need to come to Earth at the same time and there are no twin babies being born, where they can exist together, they may choose to be born in separate births, as a friend or relative, but they will become complete Soul mates.

In cases where twins are born and do not live well together, this is because these Souls have made a contract before leaving the Afterlife that they will try to exist together because of a previous conflict. This is one way they can try to solve the problem. They are so closely connected that they need to work out a solution so as to co-exist peacefully. This is also a lesson they have come to learn. Twin Souls who live in harmony are also here to learn. They don't just come to Earth to live a happy life together, otherwise there would be no point in them being here.

One twin Soul may only need to come for a very short time and this is because it only needed to learn that particular lesson in that short period of time, while the other twin Soul may need a lot longer to learn what it needs to learn. During the second Soul's lifetime on Earth it can feel the existence of the departed Soul, as they are so closely connected. They will, however, reconnect in another lifetime so as to continue their journey together.

This happens in all multiple births, some Souls may choose to come for a short period of time, while others come for a lot longer, or all the Souls may have chosen to stay for the duration of their lives. All Souls are closely connected, but multiple births have a particularly close connection and they may also need the support of their twin Soul for their journey through lifetimes together.

Purity of the Soul

———— ⊙∞⊙ ————

No matter what we do, or how we live, the Soul is always pure. The Soul is magnified to a point of brilliance when it is ready to descend to the Earth for another lifetime. We say descend to Earth even though the Afterlife is only a few feet away, because it has to come through the thin veil separating the two dimensions.

It is brilliant, revitalised, energised and ready for the journey ahead.

The Soul has no malice or ill intent. The Soul is not judgemental or cruel. It is pure from the beginning to the end. This is why we ask that humans look at the Soul, not the body, as from this we cannot judge. The body or the character may not be perfect, but the Soul is pure.

Even in the vilest of criminals lies a perfect Soul. Their misdemeanours come from a mindset brought from the other side as their chosen lifestyle, to learn what they need to learn, or to carry out a contract made with another Soul before leaving the Afterlife. This can cover a vast number of different deeds done against another. In all the Soul stays pure.

The Journey of Jesus

When the Entities began to speak of Jesus I was reluctant to write what they were giving me, but then Yellmean, Jeanette, Jeremy, Yellow Feathers and Plellal pointed out they were all poor people on Earth, as was Jesus, and it was then that I understood why they were talking of the journey of Jesus. As was written in earlier writings, some of the greatest people on Earth were poor.

(Rellman, my other Entity, said he was free from a poor existence on Earth. He lived many centuries ago and was associated with Jesus. He was one of the few rich people who supported Jesus in his quest for peace and harmony among his fellow Man.)

The passage as follows:-

We would like to speak of Jesus. Jesus was a very special Soul sent to Earth to speak to Mankind of love and forgiveness. Jesus procured John the Baptist to continue baptising people. John the Baptist was also a very special Soul, who came to Earth to teach Mankind love and forgiveness. There were other special Souls who followed, but all were persecuted and killed for their actions. This was also in the plan. They chose to come to Earth to carry out these duties and understood they would be executed for their efforts.

People are now in awe of these great men for their service to Mankind and for their sacrifice for the human race. They came to Earth for a special reason, as do all of us. They came to teach and to learn. Their purpose was more profound than most of us, but the principal of their existence was the same as ours.

Jesus was a very humble man, who took his reason for being on the Earth Plane very seriously. This was to be his last journey here, and he knew it would make such an impact that he would be remembered for evermore, so there was no need for him to come back again to live another lifetime.

The connection between Jesus and the Earth is unconditional love and understanding, and this is the lesson he hopes we can all learn.

Two Lives

We live two lives unbeknown to us. The one we have chosen to come back to Earth to live is our Spiritual life. The other is our Earthly life. They are one and the same, but we do not realise it. Mostly we keep looking for the meaning of our life and that places us at a disadvantage, not knowing why we are here. If only we could realise the life we are living is the life we are meant to live. That is why it is said we are living two lives.

The Earthly life, where we are searching, and our chosen Spiritual life are one and the same. Our true Spiritual life is being played out as it should be, but if we don't realise this we are constantly looking for answers. In short we can be quite oblivious to why we exist, whilst we are actually living the life that is mapped out for us.

Ultimately, we want people to realise through reading these books their purpose for being on Earth and save them from constantly searching for answers. Once they accept their life, and know it is as it is meant to be, from there they can begin to make the most of what they are here for.

Life is the thing we have to be most grateful for. Regardless of how we are living it, we are gaining so much wisdom and knowledge from it and that is our reward.

Memories

Memories are the blue print of who we are. Without having the knowledge we have from the Afterlife, our lives would be very bland. Whilst we are on the Earth Plane we don't consciously remember our time in the Afterlife, but it is embedded in our DNA and is there for all time. Our Soul is embedded with information for evermore.

Each time on the Earth Plane is a time to gather more information to add to the accumulation of learning we already have. We carry memories through life after life.

Whatever information we gather on Earth stays with our Soul, even though at times humans can be quite forgetful. People who suffer from Alzheimer's may forget a lot of what they have experienced on Earth, but that information stays in their DNA, to be taken with them when they leave the Earth Plane.

We may wonder why this has any importance to our lives, to know this information stays with us eternally. All information we allow ourselves to absorb over our many lifetimes makes us the complete Soul we are meant to be when we finally come home to Eternal Glory. Without this learning and knowledge we are incomplete and need to come back again and again until all is learnt. Once this is done we can rest eternally in peace and harmony.

People Who Don't Believe

---- ❦ ----

People who don't believe we have more than one life consider themselves to be the informed people and in no way will they entertain the concept that we live many lives over the time before we reach our final destination. Instead of condemning these people for their misunderstanding, we must accept that this is their chosen journey and they will ultimately learn what they have come to Earth to learn.

No Man has the right to condemn another for how they are living their life and this is probably one of the hardest lessons we as humans need to learn.

Those who do not believe we have many lives can make just as big a contribution to this life as any of us who do believe. They live their lives according to their own beliefs. Some make monumental contributions during their Earthly incarnation, while others make very little. Whichever way it is, it is that person's

personal journey and he must be left in peace
to live it.

Morals

Man lives by a different code to that which
Spirit expects of him. Man has long been told
the physical actions of a human can sometimes
be punishable by God, meaning any physical
actions by a Man or Woman, other than with
their current partner, is immoral. Morality is a
Man-made code by which he judges another,
but it is not judged by Spirit.

This does not condone the actions of one Man
against another and Man must have his own
code to live by. What is merely being explained
here is that God does not punish Man or Woman
for what they choose to do with their bodies.
This is for Man to judge, not Spirit.

This subject has been spoken of in earlier

writings, but Spirit must stress that Man must be his own judge on Man-made codes. This is not to say it is alright to condemn another for actions that we don't approve of, but it is for Man to judge his own actions. Man must be responsible for what he chooses to do with his own body, but this is not punishable by God. We learn by every deed we do and that is what we are on Earth for.

The Soul is us, and the body is a disposable carriage which enables us to live on Earth for the time we are here and which will eventually be buried in the ground when the Soul passes on. What we do with the body has no consequence in the Spirit World.

Condoning

We do not ask that the deeds of others against Man be condoned. When one person commits an indecent act against another, just because we forgive them does not mean we condone the deed. It simply means we have forgiven them. This releases us from any internal turmoil this deed has created.

Forgiving, but not condoning, allows us to carry on our life without the burden of harbouring ill feelings towards another person. Forgiving can come in many forms. We can forgive and still remember the deed, or we can forgive and allow the deed to be a distant memory. We need to find our own way of forgiving without condoning. When this is done our Soul is once again at peace.

Man can sometimes carry the burden of an act committed against him for a very long time, for at times he feels if he forgives the act, he is somehow condoning it. We want Man to know that forgiving, but not condoning, will take Man closer to his final journey home to the Spirit World. This does not mean Man will die earlier, it simply means he has learnt a monumental lesson and he may not have to come back many more times.

Please condone a wonderful, kind act towards Man, and forgive an indecent act towards Man, without condoning it.

Beyond the Grave

Many people believe that once our bodies are buried in the ground, or cremated, that that is the end of our life. It can be the end of one of our lives as we know it, but it is only one chapter in the whole scheme of things. It is like an insect shedding a shell so that it can go on to a more beautiful and productive life.

We leave the body behind as though we are disposing of a heavy cargo that has no more use to us and we are free to fly. However, we must not dismiss the body as though it is not, or has not been, very important to us. We must respect the carriage that has allowed us to live on this Earth as a human being. Once we leave the body and go beyond the grave, we must respect our bodies and all we have learnt whilst on the Earth Plane, for this is part of our path towards Eternal Glory.

Spirit would like us to respect the body while we are on the Earth Plane, for without it we could not exist. The body is a gift to us so that we can live and learn on Earth and in return we should respect it to the best of our ability and know it is only on loan for a certain period of time.

Once we have left our bodies and have gone beyond the grave, we will realise how important our carriage was and know that the next body we inhabit must also be equally important. The home of the Soul during the Earthly experience is the body and, whether it is short or long, the body is our Soul's haven until it is time to go beyond the grave.

The Human Form

⸌⸍⸌

We may wonder why we come back in the human form to continue our life on the Earth Plane. The human form is designed specifically so as to have all the functions that are needed for this Earth journey. Our bodies have been designed for any possible need we may have during our Earth lifetime.

We have also been given the five senses so as to help us on our way and, without these, life could be a lot more difficult. We must remember though, that some people have chosen to come back with some form of inability or impairment. This is the journey they have chosen so as to experience hardships and to learn from it.

This is why we ask that, if we have been born with a healthy body, to take care of it to the best of our ability. Even though some of us are destined to develop diseases as our chosen journey, if we have taken care of our bodies the chosen impairment or disease is easier to cope with. From the time we are born, until the time when we expire, our bodies keep working for us in whatever capacity they can.

The human form is a magnificently designed piece of mechanism and we must not take it lightly. We must honour it, as we must honour our life on the Earth Plane.

Double Inhabitants

Double inhabitants means in some cases two Souls will inhabit the same body, as they are both ready to come to Earth at that time and are both needing the same sort of life experiences. This body, the time, the place, the situation, are all available at the time these Souls need to inhabit.

These Souls have agreed to share the same body so as to learn what they need to learn and this is the way they have decided to do it. They may both be prepared to live in a harmonious way to learn their life's lesson. If the Souls choose to live in a non-harmonious way, this of course will affect the human who they inhabit in some detrimental way. The Souls may choose this way to learn the lesson of how to live happily together. If this is not the case, they will have to learn to co-exist somehow, which is a huge lesson within itself.

The human in which the Souls have chosen to inhabit will have an adverse experience until the Souls find a way to co-exist together. When they have done this, one Soul may choose to go back to the Afterlife because it has learnt what it has come for. This will allow the other Soul sole existence within the human body, to go on to learn what it needs to learn in the time it has chosen to be on the Earth Plane.

A conflict between the two Souls could be perceived as schizophrenia in the human body, however this is not the case. It only exhibits as schizophrenia, but is in actual fact the two Souls having a conflict within the body.

We must point out once again that the Soul is pure. These experiences are only learning curves and the Soul means no malice.

Personality of the Soul

Each Soul keeps its personality throughout each lifetime and that is how our personality is defined. We may have personality traits through the generations, as Souls mostly reincarnate into family and friends groups.

Personality comes with the Soul. It is embedded into the Soul as is DNA and memory. You may notice someone say something to the effect of: "Your grandfather used to do the same thing", so there is a possibility that you could have been your grandfather in another life. In another case we may have a similar personality to an ancestor from many generations ago, as sometimes we need to wait a long time to have the right body to reincarnate into.

When a mother loses a child, it is almost certain that child will come back into the family as part of the immediate family or extended family. Meanwhile, that child remains very close to the mother while in the Afterlife, until it is ready to reincarnate back into the fold. Whatever the case, Souls are always close. They are as close as a few feet away in the Afterlife, or as close to us as a family member or friend when reincarnated back to the Earth Plane.

Never doubt our loved ones are always near. It is the circle of life until we come to our final destination in Eternal Glory.

A Time to Unload

We gather over our lifetime many ideas, some we may learn from and some are deemed redundant thoughts. We also take on many worries and responsibilities, some we learn from and some are deemed redundant.

Throughout our lives we meet a great number of people, all with different views and outlooks. Some of these we can learn from and some we would be wise to make redundant. We make many changes in our lives; this could be the people we meet, the houses we live in, the countries we travel to, or the jobs we do. There can be a great deal of learning from these experiences, but there are also some situations we need to make redundant.

Many of us carry the burden of so many unnecessary factors in our lives because we may not have thought about the possibility of making some of these redundant and shedding unwanted burdens. There could be times in our lives when we feel so laden down with responsibilities and even people who become a burden that we may need to reassess what is valuable and what we may need to unload.

Spirit advises freedom of choice and this may mean leaving behind what is no longer valuable in our lives. We must love and care for those less fortunate than ourselves and it is natural to want to love and care for those people who are closely connected to us. Whenever these people or circumstances become a burden though, we must allow them to go, as they are on a journey of learning and cannot do so if we insist on keeping them close.

Misguided Loyalties

―――――――――― ∽∾∽ ――――――――――

When we insist on helping someone because we think they need our help and cannot do things on their own, this is what we call misguided loyalties. We feel we are being loyal to this person, or these people, by giving them a constant helping hand. We sometimes feel this person or these people cannot do without our help. We see them struggle and feel it is our duty to help them out.

This may seem like a contradiction to what has been written previously about helping people less fortunate than ourselves. However, there comes a time when we must realise that we may be retarding this person's journey by constantly bailing them out of difficult situations. If we insist on constantly helping when nothing is changing, then we must reassess our part in this person's life and realise they will be prevented from learning the lessons they have come to this Earth Plane to learn.

Sometimes the old adage of "being cruel to

be kind" can well and truly relate to this situation. We must always value our kindness in trying to help, but we must also value our intellect to know when it is time to let go.

The More Magnificent

The more magnificent we see our lives, the more magnificent our lives will be. We can only function on the level we see ourselves. If we see ourselves as underdogs or underlings, our lives will reflect that. If we see ourselves as hard done by, then our lives will also reflect that. If we see ourselves as wonderful, happy and successful people, then our lives will be a reflection of that.

This does not mean that if we see ourselves as wonderful, successful, happy people, that we are necessarily going to be financially successful, it simply means that we are going to feel successful, happy people. Every aspect of our lives is governed by how we see ourselves and how we see the world.

Many of us who are poor and have hardships in our lives can quite often be the people who see themselves as the most successful. Every little achievement these people reach is a success in their lives and that makes them happy. We may be financially successful and have every possible advantage in life, but if we don't see it that way then we are not going to be successfully happy.

The most magnificent thing we can achieve in life is the love of ourselves, the love of God and the Universe, and to appreciate this life we have been given. For without this life, we cannot be on the path to Eternal Glory.

PS. At the end of this book I was introduced to another Entity call Thelma. Thelma apparently is going to play a big part in the writing of the fifth book. I want to say I am very happy to meet her and look forward to working with her in the near future.

Please allow yourself time to process,

absorb and accept this information.

Please know this information is true and correct.

Let these Messages be consolidated
within yourself

before you move on to the next book.

———————— ⤜✦⤛ ————————

Messages From
The Spirit Realm

AN OVERVIEW OF THE AFTER LIFE

June Redfearne

Messages
from the
Spirit Realm
An Overview of the After life

Yellow Feathers, Rellman, Yellmean, Jeanette,
Jeremy, Plellal, Reokmank, Thelma and Zellan
channel these words to June for
this fifth book.

Kelly and Mertle have joined us for the last
two chapters of this book.

Please believe this information.

Please glean this information.

**Please let this information be
of great help.**

An Overview of the Afterlife

—————————— ❦ ——————————

In addition to the four previous writings channelled to June from Spirit, we would like Man to know an overview of the Afterlife, some not revealed until now.

Man walks on the Earth as Man will walk in Heaven in Spirit form. The Spirit form is allowing the Soul to move around freely with no encumbrance of the human body. This allows the shadowy Soul to be where it needs to be at any given time.

We may wonder why, when the Soul leaves the body at the time of death, we cannot see it as it ascends to the Afterlife. The Soul, accompanied by the Spirit, can ascend to the Afterlife without being seen by the human eye because we as humans are not engineered to see extra dimensional activities as they occur.

Some people may relate that they have seen a shadowy figure leave the body at the time of death, and this can be so, but it is the Spirit that can be seen on occasion, rather than the Soul.

This is a rare phenomenon. It would be fair to say that a chill may be felt in the air at the time of death and this is the precise moment that the Soul leaves the body to go on to the Afterlife.

When the Soul is expelled from the body at the time of death is when we may hear a puff, or a small gasp, from the human it has inhabited. This may be the only indication we have that the Soul has left the body, after which the body becomes limp and lifeless. The Spirit has also left the body to escort the Soul to the Afterlife. The Soul and the Spirit then pass through the thin veil separating the two dimensions, where the Soul will remain and the Spirit will return to Earth.

It will depend on how the body has expired, as to where the Soul will go initially. In a case of extreme sickness or trauma, such as murder, the Soul will firstly go to a place of peace and healing before it goes on to the Afterlife.

The Spirit will leave the Soul to heal and then it will return to Earth until such times when the Soul is ready to transcend to the Afterlife. The Spirit will then finish its job of taking the Soul to where it is meant to go.

Even though it has been healed, the memory of the trauma or sickness can stay with the Soul.

This can determine how long the Soul stays in the Afterlife before its next journey to the Earth Plane. As explained earlier, this will also depend on a suitable carriage for the Soul to exist in while on the Earth and what lessons it needs to learn.

In extreme cases, when the Soul gets lost on its way to the Afterlife, it can take a very long time for the Soul to be prepared to go back to Earth for another life. In the first place, it may take many eons for it to reach its destination and many more before it's prepared to try again. This will keep the Soul in a state of limbo for a very long time but it will eventually return to Earth for its next incarnation.

The Heart and the Brain

We may think the Soul is as big as the human Body and we may also think it would be heavy for the Spirit to transport it to the Afterlife. However, the Soul is relatively small compared to the human body. The Soul fervently encompasses itself to what we consider the core of our human body. Some people may consider the heart to be the core of our body, while others may consider the brain to be the core of our existence.

Wherever the Soul encompasses itself is where the human mainly works from. If the Soul encompasses itself around the heart, then those people act mainly from the Heart. If the Soul encompasses itself around the brain, then that is where that person mainly works from. We need people who work mainly from the heart and we need people who work mainly from the brain. This is not to say the heart or the brain person doesn't use their other thoughts and feelings, it simply means one is stronger than the other.

An example of this is that a scientist could function mainly from the brain, or a doctor or a nurse could function mainly from the heart. Those people who become very wise during their lifetime, and seem to be functioning from the brain, have earned their wisdom through life experiences and not necessarily from the brain function. These very wise people are usually heart functioning people.

These are only examples and in most cases are so, but not always, as it will depend on why these people take up these professions in the first place. Spirit could give many, many examples but it only needs a small explanation for Man to understand the concept.

A Soul can spend many centuries flowing backwards and forwards from Earth to the Afterlife with existence after existence, until it eventually reaches Utopia and has gathered all the knowledge from these many lifetimes that it needs to know.

Where the Spirit is

We may wonder where the Spirit is when the Soul has encompassed itself around the heart or the brain and we want Man to know that the Spirit flows freely through the body at all times. When the time allows, the Spirit will accompany the Soul to the Afterlife and will return to Earth until next the Soul is ready to reincarnate. It will then gather the Soul and accompany it back to Earth to be born into the chosen human being.

The Spirit plays a big part in our existence and it is good to know that the Spirit and the Soul play different parts as some people may think the Spirit and the Soul are one and the same.

The Spirit and the Soul are different components and they each play a significant role in our existence. The body may be weak but the Spirit is strong and can keep us strong in times of adversity. Also the Spirit can be what allows us to push through when we feel there is no hope. Please respect the Spirit and prevent our bodies from becoming a vessel of ill health.

The Spirit can grow weak if we allow our bodies to become unhealthy. The Spirit will fight very hard to stay strong especially in cases of ill health, such as cancer or heart disease, and this is why it is known that people may seem very strong when they are suffering and have extra strength to make themselves well again. Once the Spirit becomes weak then that is when the body is likely to expire.

When the Soul Reaches the Other Side

❧

Once the Soul reaches the other side, it will begin another journey of life in the Hereafter. It will first reunite with friends and loved ones who have gone before; it will move effortlessly among those it loves and can sometimes choose to spend the most time with a loved one who may feel the need of that Soul's presence. This may be because the two loved ones spent some time together on Earth as a couple. Where the Soul has had more than one partner on Earth it may choose to spend time with each partner.

There is no malice, hate or jealously in the Afterlife, so it is feasible for Souls to be together happily and with no judgement. After our Soul reaches the other side, and after some adjustments, it loses all prejudgements made on Earth. It loses any negative feelings and emotions it may have carried towards another human being.

This usually happens fairly quickly, unless there has been a very intense situation on Earth where two parties may have intensely disliked each other. Where one person may die before the other, the Soul who has departed first may take some time to realise their feelings and emotions towards the person still living are neither beneficial nor warranted.

When the Soul reaches the other side it may still feel as though it is in human form and, because it feels so light and unencumbered, it imagines it has been healed of all earthly problems and sicknesses. This is why the Earth people say the crippled have been healed, the sick are well and the mentally affected are at peace again. Earth people know of this because some have had communication with those in the Afterlife. In actual fact the body has been discarded at the time of death and has no bearing on the Soul any more.

Levels

There is the concept that there are several levels in the Afterlife, much like a tall building with several floors. This comes from the age-old idea that we rise higher and higher the closer we get to Utopia. In actual fact, this is correct, but we only rise as Souls in our own knowledge, wisdom and understanding. There is only one Afterlife, but there are several levels of learning and achievement.

Each journey to the Earth Plane brings us to a higher level of wisdom. Even though our lives may seem to be all problems and hardships, this is just another experience in our growth. So far, we have learnt we need experiences to grow and, because of this, Spirit would like us to accept our experiences and know they are our ticket to Eternal Glory.

Yellow Feathers (My Indian Entity) wants us to know the Indian culture keeps believing in life after death as do other indigenous cultures. This has been their belief for many, many centuries.

Their cultures are very in tune with the cycle of life and are mostly accepting of death when it comes. They are at peace with it because of their ancient knowledge and beliefs. They do mourn the death of a loved one, but they understand the process of life and death.

Most indigenous cultures are wise beyond the understanding of their white counterparts. This is not to say the white man does not understand, but with indigenous people it has been a way of life, whereas the white culture has been led by the information that has been learnt through the many different religions we have been governed by. Some of this information is not always correct.

All about Secrets of the Afterlife

The assumption that all Souls reincarnate is not correct. Some Souls prefer to reach the Afterlife and spend their duration of time without returning to the Earth Plane for another lifetime.

These Souls feel their time is better spent greeting the newly passed Souls and helping them to adjust to their new surroundings. They can also help the new Souls to meet with their previously passed family and friends. This is only in the case of a newly passed Soul being disorientated and confused as to where they are.

Those Souls who stay in the Afterlife to help new arrivals will eventually gain enough status to go on to Utopia, without having to spend any more time on the Earth Plane. These Souls are called Ready Made Angels of Infinity. They are called as such because they don't need to go back to the Earth Plane to learn more lessons; they earn their status in the Afterlife by helping others to cross peacefully and happily.

Travelling Time

We may wonder how long it takes for the Soul to reach the Afterlife once death has occurred. From the time of death to the arrival in the Afterlife is only a matter of seconds. This is why it can be quite confusing for the passed over Soul to realise it has left the body it existed in and has passed through the veil separating the two dimensions.

If a person has been suffering a long illness and has been in a lot of pain, the Soul prepares itself for departure from the body and is very happy to be going home. In this case the Soul is not confused about being in the Afterlife as it has been expecting it for a long time. In a case of sudden death the Soul can be confused as to where it is once it reaches the Afterlife, as it has not had time to prepare for its departure.

As written before, in a case of murder where the body is being put through a tremendous amount of pain and suffering, the Soul begins to prepare itself to leave the body when the pain and trauma becomes too much for the body to bear.

It is understandable that a Soul can be confused when sudden death occurs, as the transition is so quick it has not had time to prepare for its departure and suddenly finds itself in another dimension. This is where the Ready Made Angels of Infinity come into play by comforting the newly passed Soul and helping it to come to terms with this new situation.

Divine Intervention

Intervention can be from a divine source when an incident happens which could otherwise cause harm. If we are not meant to be harmed or killed at that time in our life, divine intervention will happen, meaning an Angel or Spirit will intervene and prevent us from being hurt.

We must understand there will be many accidents, mishaps and incidences during our lifetime which won't have divine intervention and this is because we cannot go through life unscathed in some shape or form. These are the hardships we learn from and we must experience these incidents throughout our lifetime. Divine intervention only happens when we need to be saved from harm so we can go on to live the life we are meant to live.

How often has it been heard that someone was saved from being killed or harmed and such incidents have been called a miracle. These interventions are carried out by what we describe as Angels of Mercy. Hopefully, by reading these books we begin to realise that there are many different Angels and Spirits who carry out a multitude of different tasks and we must realise that we are never alone.

These Angels of Mercy are called as such because they mercifully save us from being harmed if we are meant to go on living in a different way. There are Angels of Mercy, Ready Made Angels of Infinity and many more who help us through our lifetime. We just ask that you be aware of their existence and be grateful for their assistance.

Unwelcome Interference

❧❧❧

Unwelcome interference can come from a Spirit who can deliberately get in the way of the work of another Spirit. When we speak of Spirit as such, we speak of an entity that is in fact the Soul. When we speak of the Soul as being pure this is so, but for some time such Souls can be disruptive in their duties and can cause some chaos.

The reason this can happen is because the Soul feels it can sometimes know better and can act accordingly, or it may feel it has been given an unfair duty to perform. These are the Souls who have had very few experiences of life and need to learn some lessons and wisdom. Even though the Soul is pure, it can be like a naughty child and can need more experiences and lessons to understand its role in the big picture of life and the Afterlife.

They can at times be instrumental in another Soul becoming lost on its way to the Afterlife. We know this can happen to a Soul if the Spirit is not strong enough to do its job of taking the Soul to the Afterlife, but interference can also come from an inexperienced Soul and it can cause some distress.

When a newly passed Soul is about to enter the Afterlife, an inexperienced Soul can interfere with the newly passed Soul's journey and can cause it to lose its way into the Afterlife. This can cause some havoc with the Spirit trying to do its duty. These inexperienced Souls will soon learn their place and can be instrumental in guiding other inexperienced Souls at a later date.

Omens from the Afterlife

An Omen is a warning of an upcoming occurrence, either good or bad. Spirit has spoken before of the help that is available to us when we need comfort or assurance. All we need to do is ask and help will come in some form or other. However, when it is spoken of Omens, this is another way of Spirit helping us and working to inform us of an upcoming occurrence. These occurrences can be for our good, to warn us of an event that may cause us happiness or harm.

The reason there are Omens given to us is to prevent us going on a different path to the one we are meant to be on. In other words, if we do not get these Omens, we may do some-thing differently to what we should be doing and how we should be living our lives according to the big plan. When we receive an Omen of an upcoming occurrence we should wisely con-sider this sign and act accordingly and this will keep us on our God-given course.

This once again proves that Spirit has our best interest at heart and is always looking out for us. We may be going through some hard times and feel as though the Omen given to us is of no benefit to us at all. However, we are on the path we are meant to be on and we need to be on that path so as to learn and grow the way we are meant to learn and grow.

Please take notice of Omens and signs. These are in our best interest and they come from Angels, who are referred to as Angels of Information and Protection.

The Power of Belief

The Power of belief is the strongest power we have. The power of belief can hold us in good stead in any situation and, even though we are destined to live the life we have chosen to live, the power of belief can bring us through it under any circumstances. When we have the power of belief we have connected into the Angels and it is from there that we will prevail.

The power of belief may not take us the way we think it will, but it will take us the way it is meant to take us. When we ask the Angels for help, they will take us in the way that is in our best interest. Although we may feel it is not working, it will be the best outcome. The power of belief is like believing in the Angels and therefore the Angels have our permission to help us out.

If only we humans could realise the power we have within us, and the good that could come from it, there would be less anger and frustration and more peace and harmony on Earth. We hold so much power in our hands that is a gift from the Afterlife, which could make amazing things happen on Earth for the good of all humanity. Unfortunately, many of us don't tap into the power we have and therefore miss the opportunity of making our lives better.

Please know the power is within us. This is the power of the Angels, so please believe.

Angels Who Come and Go

These Angels are called Transitional Angels, who are given the job of transcending the thin veil when the need arises. These are especially chosen Angels because of the sometimes difficult task they have to perform.

When a Soul leaves the Earth Plane for the Afterlife, it has as much time as is needed to adjust and enough time to decide when to reincarnate. However, the Transitional Angels have the job of coming back through the thin veil when they are called upon and this can sometimes be quite difficult because of the extreme change in the dimensions. This is why they have been especially chosen for this job.

When we are in desperate need of help and we call upon the Angels, these are the Angels who transition to the Earth Plane to help us out. We must remember that Angels will not interfere unless we ask for their help, or if we have total belief. Total belief is like connecting to the Angels, therefore it is considered a request for help.

These Angels also choose not to reincarnate as they will constantly be gaining wisdom from their many, many entries through the thin veil back to the Earth Plane when their help is needed.

As spoken in earlier writings, we may consider a small miracle has occurred when we need some guidance or help and this is where these wonderful Transitional Angels come into play. They may show up in the form of a person and then disappear as fast as they came, or some small event may occur that is very beneficial to our cause. This is also the work of the Transitional Angels.

We have tried to instil many times through these writings to have faith and to trust there is help and guidance available for when it is needed. All we have to do is believe and to ask.

Souls at War

War has a very different meaning in the Afterlife than it does on Earth. War in the Afterlife means Working at Reconciliation and many Souls who have been at war on the Earth Plane have to work very hard towards reconciliation in the Afterlife. The main objective is to reconcile with those who have been their bitter enemies on Earth because this is part of the process of growth and one very hard lesson for the previously embittered Souls to learn.

These Souls soon realise, had it not been for the choices of others, some of these could have become friends on the Earth Plane and that their embattlement on Earth was part of a plan from the Afterlife before coming to Earth. When this is known, the Souls will then become reconciled and would have learnt a very great lesson.

There are many ways Souls need to reconcile after reaching the Afterlife. One is where one Soul has murdered the other while on the Earth and for many other reasons. Much of this has been explained in earlier writings and when things become clear the Souls involved will realise this was all predestined and will eventually thank their previous perpetrator for the part they played in carrying out their role while on the Earth Plane.

This is where the Souls, The Ready Made Angels of Infinity, who have chosen to stay in the Afterlife and not return to Earth, come into play, by helping those embittered Souls to come to terms with their experiences on Earth and to be at peace.

The Afterlife is all about love and peace, reconciliation and growth. The fact that the transition from Earth to the Afterlife is so quick, it doesn't give the Soul time to process all this before arriving in the Afterlife. This is why it all has to be resolved once they reach their destination.

❦

Rose Garden of the Afterlife

———————— ⟨⟩ ————————

When we speak of roses we think of beautiful colours and exotic smells, but this is only the tip of the iceberg to how the colours and aromas are in the Afterlife. The magnificence of the Afterlife cannot be compared to any place on the Earth Plane. It is magnificent beyond compare. There is a whole new world functioning beyond the thin veil separating the two dimensions of the Afterlife and the Earth Plane.

Part of the growth of the Soul is choosing to come back to Earth for another incarnation. This is a hard choice to make because of the beauty and peace of the Afterlife, but one that has to be made if the Soul wants to learn and grow and go on to a higher level. The power of colour and smell can be intoxicating and something that would be very hard to leave behind.

It is so beautiful that the Souls move and float among a haze of colour and smell, peace and tranquillity, and it is in their best interest to sort out any disagreements they have brought from the Earth Plane as quickly as possible.

At first these disagreements seem irrelevant because of the speed the Soul reaches the Afterlife after death and initially it can feel almost like they are still in human form. In time this will all dispel and fall away allowing the Soul the peace and tranquillity of the home to where it has yearned to be.

Guardian Angels

We have all heard about us having a Guardian Angel and from this we all surmise we each have our own personal

Guardian Angel to take care of us.

This can seem so when we are in trouble and a small miracle occurs to help us out of it, but in actual fact, depending on the circumstance, we are being helped by an Angel of Mercy, an Angel of Information and Protection, an Angel of Infinity, a Transitional Angel and many more. This is their role and they are there when we need them. This does not necessarily mean we each have our own personal Guardian Angel. Each Angel has a specific role to play and will do so when the circumstances require.

Even with all this help, our lives will still be on the track they are meant to be on, but these Angels can make it so much easier for us if we open our hearts and believe. Keep in mind these Angels are always there to help, but unless we open our hearts and minds, we will miss any assistance they give us and may make us think the help is not there and is not possible.

We talk a lot about Angels and Guides, which are one and the same except they play different roles, in the hopes that Man can finally understand that they do exist and can be a great comfort to us.

In some circumstances one of the Angels we refer to as a Guardian Angel can be with us for a duration of time, trying to get us to understand and to tap into the help that is available. There is only a certain amount they can do and, if we are completely shut off, it will be very hard for us to notice any help at all.

In some cases, where a sudden incident may occur and it could change the course of our life when it is not meant to, an Angel will step in without being asked, because in that instance, our mind could be so open with no thoughts at all, that the Angel has time to step in before any negative thoughts return.

Ghosts

There have been many stories of ghosts seen on Earth. A lot of these happenings are in old buildings, prisons and graveyards. At times they have been seen as a smoky shape of a human and other times sounds can be heard that are not normally there.

When we see a ghostly shape this is usually the Spirit of the person who has departed. As we now know the Spirit of the person stays on Earth until the Soul is ready, once again, to rein-carnate back to the Earth Plane and the Spirit still carries the energies and personality of the departed person.

If the Spirit has not completed its job of taking the Soul to the Afterlife, the Soul can be lost for a very long time. It is on these occasions that a Spirit can be seen as a ghost around the living in the hope that it will attract enough attention so as to make the human realise a Soul is lost, and will help and encourage it to go to the light and to go home.

Ghosts are another way of letting us know there is another life after our death on the Earth Plane and, as afraid of them as we may be, they are a positive sign for us to know there is more to life than just living on Earth. A ghost can also be a comforting way of letting us know our loved ones are still around us. Whether we know it or not we walk among Spirits everyday of our lives. They are around us everywhere we are and everywhere we go and it is comforting at times to see a ghost and know how close our loved ones are.

A ghost or a smoky form of a human does not always appear to the relatives of the departed. The ghost may appear in a place where it has been familiar when living on Earth, or it may be attracted to someone it feels can help its Soul pass over to the Afterlife.

Please be aware of these ghostly figures and help in any way possible. Please do not be afraid.

Communication with Spirit

Many people can communicate with Spirit and many can help a lost Soul to pass over by directing them to go to the white light and therefore be met by family and friends. We already know the Soul goes to the Afterlife and the Spirit returns to Earth, so we may now wonder when a Medium is communicating with somebody from the other side, is it the Spirit or the Soul they are communicating with?

We want Man to know the Medium is communicating with the Spirit of the passed over person. At times a Spirit can enter the body of a Medium and is able to bring messages from the other side by using the Medium's body and voice to relate any information it may need to. This can only happen if the Medium is open to this and allows it to happen. Not all Mediums have this ability; their main job is to get messages through telepathically without necessarily having the Spirit enter their body.

As you can now see, there are several ways of being able to communicate with our loved ones and it is comforting to know they are always near.

Many, Many Lives

We would like Man to understand how we as Souls evolve. We may live many hundreds of lives in our journey to full evolvement and our eventual arrival in Utopia. Each life we live adds to our vast wisdom and knowledge.

We start off as a new undeveloped Soul in our first life as we know it and the more lives we have the more we learn. It is important to know that we do have many, many lives, as some people believe we only exist once on Earth and that it is the first and last time we are here. We must also realise that as many lives we live on Earth, we also live that many lives in the Afterlife.

It is also important to know that we existed in many different forms. We could have been man or woman, we could have been crippled or insane, and we could have been black or white or many other variations of existence. This is another reason why we must be aware of not criticising or demeaning another person for not being perfect in our eyes, because at some time during one of our lives we could have been just like the person we are mocking.

We must be so grateful for the many, many opportunities of so many different lives and so many different experiences and, although we cannot remember them whilst on Earth, we certainly remember them when we reach the other side. We also remember the reasons we went through those lives and what benefits we have gained from them. We want Man to know every lifetime is extremely valuable, so please appreciate the one you are living now. Make the most of it and know it is a very valuable step towards complete happiness.

Soul Mates

Soul Mates as we know them are Mates of the Soul. Any person we meet and feel as though they are a Soul Mate is because this arrangement has been made in the Afterlife before descending to Earth. Some people think we are destined to meet only one Soul Mate in this lifetime, and this can be true in many cases, but there are also cases of meeting more than one Soul Mate.

A Soul Mate doesn't always have to be a partner; a Soul Mate can be a friend, a family member or someone you have an instant feeling of connection and familiarity with. Many

Souls, who have been partners in a previous existence, can decide to come to Earth as best friends, or a family member, so as to experience what it is like to live a life with that person other than being a partner.

We may also meet more than one Soul Mate as a partner in this lifetime. This could be because our first Soul Mate may choose to only live a short time on Earth for whatever reason they need and then go back to the Afterlife and that allows us to meet our next Soul Mate.

Contrary to belief, a Soul Mate can also be a partner who treats us badly during our time together. This is because a contract has been made between the two Souls to come to Earth and live this existence, so as to learn a very valuable lesson that we may not otherwise have learnt. When this lesson is learnt the two Souls may part and go on to live another existence with somebody else.

This will reiterate the reason we are here on Earth, to learn and to gain knowledge. We can sometimes choose to do it in a very hard way but the rewards outweigh the event.

In another instance we can meet a Soul Mate earlier in life and spend some time together. This may be a short relationship, as we may both have lessons to learn and need to go on different paths to learn them. The reason for the early connection is that we may be meant to co-exist later on in life and we would otherwise never have met them if we had not had an earlier connection. This is like an investment in life.

Nourishment for the Soul

So far, we have spoken of the Soul's journey of living, learning, gaining wisdom and hardship. We now want to speak of nourishment for the Soul. When we speak of nourishment for the Soul, we speak of ways we as humans can feed our Soul to keep it healthy and more able to cope with the life it has ahead. Nothing is going to change the life we have mapped out for ourselves, but we can help by feeding the Soul in a way that we are more able to cope.

The first thing we need to do is to feed the Soul with love. In other words we must try to love ourselves no matter what challenges we are facing in life. In particular, if someone else feels the need to criticize or humiliate us in some form, this is the time we especially need to love ourselves more. Please remember these criticisms are only what someone else thinks and have no bearing on how we should feel about ourselves. Please know this is our life, our body, our Soul and no matter what anybody else says or does to demean us, it cannot destroy us forever if we don't allow it to.

Another way we can feed the Soul is to eat healthy and respect the body we have been given. We can feed the Soul by being in fresh air and among nature. We can feed the Soul by looking at beauty, cradling a baby, or smelling a beautiful scent. There are many and varied ways we can feed the Soul and in doing so we are feeding ourselves to a better way to live and to feel.

Different Colours

———————— ⤭ ————————

We may wonder how, and also why, people are born of different colours. There are many different colours and cultures on the Earth Plane and these all did not come from Adam and Eve. We speak of Adam and Eve because it is not in Man's best interest to teach people that civilisation began with these two people.

How Man began would be too difficult to explain and therefore we can only say there is no beginning and no end. There is an infinity about the human race that cannot be comprehended and it is not necessary for Man to know whilst on the Earth Plane. This can be one of the secrets of the Afterlife which can only be learned once reaching the other side. How Man was created in different colours is also a secret of the Afterlife but the reason for the existence of so many colours and cultures is that Man can learn from, and learn to tolerate, those others who are not the same as we are.

Man has learnt throughout the ages to put

labels on things he doesn't quite understand, but whilst on Earth Man does not have the capabilities to understand the workings of the Afterlife. Man may speak of God, Adam and Eve and many of the great people of history, but he must understand that life did not begin there.

Possessions

Some people may gauge their worth by the possessions they have acquired and some may think they are above everyone by what they own. In the first instance, credit must be given to those who have worked very hard and have acquired many things. However, these do not make a person better or more valuable than anyone else. In actual fact Earth has become a very materialistic place and Man can be driven to gain more and more.

This subject has been touched on in earlier

writings and it must be reiterated that possessions do not make the Man. If only we realised how little we need to survive and that the greatest gifts we can acquire are love, compassion and wisdom. These are far more valuable possessions and these are what make the Man.

Some of us may be generous with our possessions, while others can become jealous and possessive of what they own. We must realise these things are inanimate objects and cannot be taken with us when we pass over to the other side. However, our love, compassion and wisdom can. We can also leave these gifts behind with the people we love, to add to the memory of their departed loved one.

One huge possession we have acquired is the acquisition of the Earth and this is a responsibility we all must take seriously. We must learn to share and care for the land we live in. We must care for the people we love and who love us, and we must share our love and compassion with the world to make it a better place.

Baby Souls

⤜ ✤ ⤛

We would like to talk about Souls of babies who pass prematurely. Some of these can be from abortion, stillbirths or babies passing very young. These Souls of the very young, who have returned to the Afterlife before barely spending any time on the Earth Plane, are nurtured by very special Angels called Angels of Nurturing. Although these Souls may have spent many lifetimes on Earth prior, they are in their infancy in this lifetime and therefore are considered very young Souls.

These Souls may have other loved ones in the Afterlife such as grandparents, but mostly they are without their mother to whom they were entrusted. This then becomes the responsibility of the Angels of Nurturing. These Angels are once again chosen for their very special role. Even though these Souls have chosen to come to Earth for a very short time, their passing can sometimes be traumatic and therefore need special nurturing by these very special Angels.

The Souls of these very young babies are cared for in a crèche like situation until they are strong enough to be cared for by an already passed relative. Likewise, small children who have passed are cared for by Angels called Angels of Mothering, until such times as they are strong enough to be cared for by a relative. We would like mothers of babies and young children to know that they are being nurtured and mothered and cared for in a most comforting way until they are once again reunited with their mother.

In another instance these Souls may choose to come back to Earth very soon after and can be born to the same mother and live a long and happy life. Whatever way it is, they have come for a purpose which has been met and they are happy to return to the Afterlife.

A Time to Reflect

﹏﹏﹏﹏﹏﹏ ❧❧ ﹏﹏﹏﹏﹏﹏

There are many times in our lives when it would be in our best interest to reflect. This means to stop and think and look back over what has been in our lives and consider if what we are doing, or have done, is where we want to be. Spirit has given Man many tools in these writings to look at life in a different way and help him understand the reasons Man is on Earth and the complexity of life.

We may consider imagining looking into a pond and seeing our reflection and asking ourselves if the person we see looking back at us is the person we want to be. We may consider trying to see ourselves through the eyes of others and imagine what they see and use them as we would a pond to check our reflection. This method could be used as our personal way to reflect on our behaviour and way of life.

Our opinion of ourselves is the only one that counts and, if this opinion is a disparaging one, then we must alter the way we think of ourselves. In some cases this opinion can be changed by changing our actions and, in other cases, we must try to learn to love ourselves, for what we are is what we are meant to be and this is a beautiful Soul in the eyes of the Universe. We are a beautiful Soul, educated, wise, passionate, loving and glorious. If only Man could keep that in mind, then all else would fade away. Please reflect to others.

The Meaning for Life

For many centuries the age-old question has been: what is the meaning for life, why are we here and would it make a difference if we never existed? We are not talking of the meaning OF life, but we are talking of the meaning FOR life, the reason there is life.

Once again Man needs to go beyond the Earth, back to the Afterlife, before any comprehension of the beginning of life can be learnt. It can only be explained in simple terms that since we do exist, there must be a destination to head for, otherwise life would have no meaning. Our destination is Utopia and we are trying to teach Man the many steps and about the lives we have to go through to reach the ultimate destination.

When a Soul embarks on the journey of life from the beginning, it cannot take on the burden of knowing every step and every life it needs to go through, otherwise it would never embark on it in the first place. A Soul will live a life and then go back to the Afterlife before it can decide whether to, or when, it will start the process all over again with another life.

Let not the burden of our journey consume us. Let the wonderment of life surround us.

Miracle of Life

⸎

There is nothing more meaningful than the miracle of life. This covers all forms of life, including animals and vegetation, all created in this thing we call the image of the Universe.

Man has the knowledge of how he was created but it is hidden deep within the subconscious and can only be remembered after reaching the other side of the thin veil separating the two dimensions called the Afterlife. Many people will refer to this as Heaven, as this could possibly be their only knowledge of the name for the Afterlife.

Perhaps Man can begin to comprehend the miracle of life now that these facts have been revealed, the miracle of life and the Life After. Man is connected to the Afterlife as a baby is connected to the mother by the umbilical cord. Even though the cord is cut, the connection is never broken.

Spirit cannot emphasise more the miracle of life and how Man needs to value his life as something precious rather than something that just happens.

Let This Not Be the End

Spirit has armed Man with much information throughout these writings. Let not this be read and forgotten. Let this be the starting point of Man's education of life on Earth and in the Afterlife. Let these words be the springboard of our learning and let it not be forgotten the good Man can do for the Earth and for each other.

We bless each and every Man. We follow Man's every byway and highway until the path ends and Man comes home to the Afterlife and Eternal Glory.

All Encompassed

--- ❧ ---

Some finals words from Yellow Feathers:
We are ALL encompassed with the knowledge of these books. We can now perhaps look in another direction to where we were going. We can perhaps understand more of the process of life and the journey we have embarked upon. Therefore, with more understanding, we can be more accepting of our situations here on Earth.

We now know this is only one of many lives we are to lead and, with each time on Earth, we learn more and gain more wisdom. These are the essential points of existence and why we are here. It is not for us to earn more money and to be better than the next Man. It is not for us to display our wealth and therefore feel superior to others less fortunate than ourselves. It is not to criticise and demean Mankind because they may not have as much as we have, or they may not be as intelligent or look as good as we do.

We must realise that we are all at our own

stage of growth and must be accepted for where we are and how far we have come. We must show compassion where it is needed and be wise enough to know when to let go.

Message from Spirit:-

Yellow Feathers wants June to know these books are finished.

Rellman wants June to know Spirit is very much grateful to June for writing these five books and wants to thank June for June's patience and time to write these books. Mertle wants June to know Kelly and Mertle are very pleased to become June's friends forever.

www.ingramcontent.com/pod-product-compliance
Lightning Source LLC
Chambersburg PA
CBHW041819090426
42811CB00009B/1039